The Encyclopedia of
North American Indians

Volume VI

Iowa Indians – McIntosh, William

General Editor
D. L. Birchfield

Marshall Cavendish
New York • London • Toronto

Published in 1997 by
Marshall Cavendish Corporation
99 White Plains Road
Tarrytown, NY 10591-9001
U.S.A.

Developed, designed, and produced by Water Buffalo Books, Milwaukee

Project director: Mark J. Sachner
General editor: D. L. Birchfield
Art director: Sabine Beaupré
Photo researcher: Diane Laska
Project editor: Valerie J. Weber

Editors: Elizabeth Kaplan, MaryLee Knowlton, Judith Plumb, Carolyn Kott Washburne

Consulting editors: Donna Beckstrom, Jack D. Forbes, Annette Reed Crum, John Bierhorst

Picture credits: © B. & C. Alexander: 738; © Archive Photos: 736, 740, 751, 773, 776, 778, 791, 800, 821, 829, 836, 839, 844, 853, 854, 864; © Kit Breen: 762, 769, 783, 851; © Corbis-Bettmann: 725, 735, 766, 779, 782, 789, 815, 823, 835, 843, 845, 849, 850, 860; Photo © Addison Doty, Courtesy of Morning Star Gallery: 807 (both); © Steven Ferry: 793; © William B. Folsom 1991: 837; © Porter Gifford/Gamma Liaison: 796; © Hampton University Archives, Hampton, Virginia: 726, 756, 792 (both), 794; © Hazel Hankin: 737, 801, 802; © Richard Hunt: 833, 856, 857, 858, 859; © 1994 Millie Knapp: 727, 728, 840; Photo courtesy of Milwaukee County Historical Society: 760; © Linda J. Moore: 842; © Sally Myers Photography 1995: 744; © Tom Myers Photography 1995: 742; © Antonio Pérez/¡EXITO!: 803; © Paul M. Perez: 804, 805; Provincial Archives of Manitoba: Indians — Chippewa 2 (N13342) Photograph by J. H. Clarke: 846; Rare Books and Manuscripts Division, The New York Public Library, Astor, Lenox and Tilden Foundations: 799; © Jim Rementer: 809, 810, 811, 812; © Elliott Smith: 768; © STOCK MONTAGE, INC.: 759, 771, 830; © Stephen Trimble: title, 731, 732, 743, 746, 747, 748, 754, 761, 763, 767, 770, 785, 786, 787, 797; Courtesy of the University of Oklahoma: 775; © UPI/Corbis-Bettmann: 781 (both), 819, 828, 841, 848; © 1992 S. Kay Young: Cover

Library of Congress Cataloging-in-Publication Data

The encyclopedia of North American Indians.
     p. cm.
     Includes bibliographical references and index.
     Summary: A comprehensive reference work on the culture and history of Native Americans.
     ISBN 0-7614-0233-0 (vol. 6)   ISBN 0-7614-0227-6 (lib. bdg.: set)
     1. Indians of North America--Encyclopedias, Juvenile.
[1. Indians of North America--Encyclopedias.]
E76.2.E53   1997
970.004'97'003--dc20

            96-7700
            CIP
            AC

Printed and bound in the Italy

Title page illustration: Hand-crafted silver and turquoise from Zuni Pueblo.

Editor's note: Many systems of dating have been used by different cultures throughout history. *The Encyclopedia of North American Indians* uses B.C.E. (Before Common Era) and C.E. (Common Era) instead of B.C. (Before Christ) and A.D. (Anno Domini, "In the Year of the Lord") out of respect for the diversity of the world's peoples.

Contents

IOWA INDIANS

The Iowas, who call themselves Pahodje ("snow covered"), were located in Minnesota when they first made contact with French explorers in 1701. Before settling in Minnesota, the Iowas had left their original country, which was north of the Great Lakes, in Canada, to live near the mouth of Rock River in Illinois. They began migrating again before settling in Minnesota.

In 1815, the Iowas first entered into a treaty relationship with the United States government. In 1824, the Iowas ceded their lands in Missouri to the United States, and in 1836, they were assigned a reservation along the Missouri River in Kansas. There, they lived in comfortable houses and worked profitable farms.

When, like other tribes, they were forced to give up tribal lands and accept individual allotments of land, their lands in Kansas were ceded to the United States. They then headed for Indian Territory (present-day Oklahoma), where, in 1883, the government assigned them to a reservation. They were allotted lands in 1890 through the Severalty Act, and their surplus lands, lands that were not allotted to individuals of the Iowa Nation, were opened up for settlement.

In addition to farming the land, the Iowas were skilled in many areas that made them popular trading partners with other Indian nations and with non-Native settlers. The Iowas made pipes from the red pipestone in Minnesota and were excellent in dressing buffalo skins and other animal pelts. Trading with other Indian nations gave the Iowas an advantage when settlers began moving into the area. They could then trade with the settlers and often acted as trading mediators for other tribal nations. At the time their reservation was opened for settlement, almost all Iowas could read, write, and speak English, even though more than half their population was full-blood.

The Iowas were closely allied with the Sac and Fox, with whom they had migrated from their homeland north of the Great Lakes. When the Iowas were forced to settle in Indian Territory, they went to the Sac and Fox agency first. Today, many Iowas live in northeastern Kansas near the Kansas-Nebraska state line.

The Iowa tribe became federally recognized in the late 1930s after adopting a constitution and bylaws. Although small in number, Iowas have managed to maintain much of their tribal customs and traditions throughout the invasion of settlers on their property.

SEE ALSO:

Dawes Commission; General Allotment Act; Iowa, State of; Kansas; Sac and Fox.

Iowa tribal leader White Cloud, as painted by George Catlin.

IOWA, STATE OF

Iowa, which became a U.S. state in 1846, was named after an Indian nation that had once lived within the state's borders. The name Iowa is a corrupted version of the Sioux word *Ayuhwa*, which means "Sleepy Ones." The Iowas, who call themselves Pahodje (snow-covered),were related to the Oto and Missouri tribes, who were all descended from the Winnebagos.

In addition to its name, Iowa has many connections with Native Americans. Archaeological evidence indicates that Paleo-Indians inhabited Iowa as far back as thirteen thousand years ago. Later, from 500 B.C.E. to 800 C.E., the Oneonta people of the Mississippian Culture lived in Iowa and constructed the effigy mounds. Each year, thousands of people visit Effigy Mounds Park in northeastern Iowa and are amazed by the huge burial structures in the shapes of birds and animals.

At the time of European contact, many tribes lived in Iowa. The Illinois occupied the southeastern tip of the state. The Iowa tribe had been forced out of Iowa by the Sac and Fox tribes who battled the Santee and Yankton peoples for con-

trol of the area. Fort Atkinson was built and garrisoned from 1840 to 1849 to maintain a "peace zone" between these warring tribes. Fort Atkinson was the only military fort built in the United States for the purpose of protecting Indians. A reconstruction of the fort stands at the fort's original site near Decorah, Iowa. Later, in 1857, northwestern Iowa was the site of the Spirit Lake Massacre.

The only Indian reservation in Iowa is that of the Sac and Fox peoples. The reservation covers 9,479 acres (3,792 hectares) near Tama, Iowa. The 1990 U.S. Census lists 7,349 Indians as Iowa residents, which makes Iowa fortieth among U.S. states in Native American population.

SEE ALSO:
Iowa Indians; Sac and Fox.

IROQUOIS CONFEDERACY

The Iroquois Confederacy was founded by the prophet Deganawidah, who is called "the Peacemaker" in the oral tradition of the Iroquois, with

Hampton Institute in Virginia, 1892. In that year, students from the Cayuga, Mohawk, Oneida, Onondaga, Seneca, and Tuscarora nations, of the Iroquois Confederacy (shown here), constituted the second-largest group of Indian students at Hampton.

Iroquois delegate Jay Clause participating in a public ceremony in New York in November 1994.

the help of Aionwantha, who is also popularly known as Hiawatha. The confederacy was founded, possibly as early as 900 C.E. or as late as 1500 C.E., before first European contact in the area that makes up much of the northeastern United States, principally New York State, and parts of southeastern Canada. Deganawidah's goal in forming the confederacy was to replace blood feuds among the various nations with peaceful means of decision making. The result of his work was the Great Law of Peace of the Iroquois, which survives to this day as one of the oldest forms of participatory democracy in the world. The Iroquois Confederacy originally included the Mohawks, Oneidas, Onondagas, Cayugas, and Senecas. The sixth nation, the Tuscaroras, migrated into Iroquois country in the early 1700s from what is today North Carolina.

After the coming of Deganawidah and Hiawatha and their Great Law of Peace, the Iroquois have been united by a desire to live in harmony with each other for most of their history. Called the Iroquois by the French and the Five (later Six) Nations by the English, the original tribes of the confederacy—the Mohawks, Oneidas, Onondagas, Cayugas, and Senecas—call themselves the Haudenosaunee; the word is Iroquois for "People of the Longhouse."

Each of the five Iroquois nations in the confederacy maintained its own council. Its sachems were nominated by the clan mothers of families holding hereditary rights to office titles; the clan mothers also polled the families in order to reach a consensus. Rights, duties, and qualifications of sachems were explicitly outlined, and the women could remove (or impeach) a sachem who was found guilty of any of a number of abuses of office, from missing meetings to murder. An erring chief was summoned to face charges by the war chiefs, who acted in peacetime as the people's eyes and

Iroquois celebrate the two hundredth anniversary of the Canandaigua Treaty, on the steps of the Ontario County Court House in Canandaigua, New York.

Sachems were not allowed to name their own successors, nor could they carry their titles to the grave. The traditional headdress of an Iroquois leader includes deer antlers, which are said to have been "knocked off" if the person is impeached. A chief could also be "dehorned" if he engaged in violent behavior. The Great Law also provided a ceremony to remove the antlers of authority from a dying chief and for the removal from office of sachems who could no longer adequately function in office. This measure is remarkably similar to a constitutional amendment adopted in the United States during the late twentieth century providing for the removal of an incapacitated president.

The chiefs' duties were clear: They must be "a mentor for the people at all times" and always strive to maintain peace within the league. The chiefs of the league were instructed to take criticism honestly, to have skins that "shall be seven spans thick." They were instructed to think of the coming generations in all of their actions. The law pointed out that sachems should take pains not to become angry when people scrutinized their conduct in governmental affairs. Such a point of view pervades the writings of Thomas Jefferson and Benjamin Franklin.

The Grand Council at Onondaga was drawn from the individual national councils. The Grand Council could also nominate sachems outside the hereditary structure, based on merit alone. These sachems, called "pine tree chiefs," were said to have sprung from the body of the people as the symbolic Great White Pine springs from the earth. The

ears in the council, somewhat as the role of the press was envisaged by Jefferson and other founders of the United States. A sachem was given three warnings, then removed from the council if he did not mend his ways. A sachem guilty of murder lost not only his title, but also deprived his entire family of its right to representation. The women relatives holding the rights to the office were symbolically "buried," and the title transferred to a sister family.

Great Tree was a living thing; its roots and branches were said to grow to bring in other peoples to its ways of peace.

Each nation's council sends delegates to a central council, much as each U.S. state has its own legislature, as well as senators and representatives who travel to the central seat of government in Washington, D.C. When representatives of the Iroquois nations meet in Onondaga, they form two groups: the Elder Brothers (Mohawks, Onondagas, and Senecas) and the Younger Brothers (Cayugas and Oneidas). At Onondaga, the site of the struggle with Tadadaho, a legendary evil wizard subdued by Hiawatha, the Iroquois built a perpetual council fire, "The Fire That Never Dies." The Onondagas are the Firekeepers. (In the U.S. Congress, this position is held by the Speaker of the House.)

As it was designed by Deganawidah, the procedure for debating policies of the confederacy begins with the Mohawks and Senecas (collectively called, with the Onondagas, the Elder Brothers). After being debated by the Keepers of the Eastern Door (Mohawks) and the Keepers of the Western Door (Senecas), the question is then thrown across the fire to the Oneida and Cayuga statesmen (the Younger Brothers) for discussion in much the same manner. Once consensus is achieved among the Oneidas and the Cayugas, the discussion is then given back to the Senecas and Mohawks for confirmation. Next, the question is laid before the Onondagas for their decision.

At this stage, the Onondagas have a power similar to judicial review; they can raise objections to the proposed measure if they believe it is inconsistent with the Great Law. Essentially, the legislature can rewrite the proposed law on the spot so that it can be in accord with the constitution of the Iroquois. When the Onondagas reach consensus, their ceremonial leaders, known as Tadadaho and Honowireton, confirm the decision that has been reached after the delegations have concluded their debates. Finally, Honowireton or Tadadaho gives the decision of the Onondagas to the Mohawks and the Senecas so that the policy may be announced to the Grand Council as its will. This process reflects the emphasis of the league on checks and balances, public debate, and consensus. The overall intent of such a parliamentary procedure is to encourage unity at each step.

The Iroquois have built certain ways of doing business into their Great Law to prevent anger and frayed tempers. For example, to allow time for passions to cool, an item may not be debated the same day it is first brought up. All important decisions must take at least two days, to allow leaders to "sleep on it" and not to react too quickly. The Great Law may be amended just as one adds beams to the rafters of an Iroquois longhouse.

Deganawidah's Great Law also included provisions guaranteeing freedom of religion and the right of redress before the Grand Council. It also forbade unauthorized entry of homes—all measures that sound familiar to United States citizens through the Bill of Rights.

The Iroquois also are linked to each other by their clan system, which meant that each person had family in every other nation of the federation. If a Mohawk of the Turtle Clan had to travel, he would be cared for by Turtles in the other nations.

The Iroquois Confederacy was well known to the British and French colonists of North America because of its pivotal position in diplomacy between the colonists, as well as among other Native confederacies. It controlled the only relatively level land pass between the English colonies on the seaboard and the French settlements in the Saint Lawrence Valley.

The league fractured badly during the American Revolution, when a majority of its members supported the British and a minority supported the American patriots. The Iroquois allies of the British suffered greatly at the hands of George Washington and his troops.

The Grand Council survives, however, and still meets in a simple log house on the Onondaga territory near Syracuse, New York. There, Jake Thomas, a Cayuga, spends two or three days every five years reciting the complete Great Law of Peace and its origin story. He is the only person alive late in the twentieth century who knows all of a story that has been compared to the epics of the Greek poet Homer.

— B. E. Johansen

SEE ALSO:

American Revolution; Deganawidah; Franklin, Benjamin; Hiawatha; Jefferson, Thomas; Mohawk; Oneida; Onondaga; Tuscarora.

SUGGESTED READINGS:

Arden, Harvey. "The Fire That Never Dies." *National Geographic* (September 1987): 374–403.

Bruchac, Joseph. *Iroquois Stories*. Trumansburg, NY: Crossing Press, 1985.

Caduto, Michael J., and Joseph Bruchac. *Keepers of the Earth: Native American Stories and Environmental Activities for Children*. Golden, CO: Fulcrum, 1988.

Colden, Cadwallader. *The History of the Five Nations Depending on the Province of New York in America* [1727, 1747]. Ithaca, NY: Cornell University Press, 1958.

Grinde, Donald, Jr., and Bruce E. Johansen. *Exemplar of Liberty: Native America and the Evolution of Democracy*. Los Angeles: University of California–Los Angeles, 1991.

Johansen, Bruce E. *The Forgotten Founders: Benjamin Franklin, the Iroquois and the Rationale for the American Revolution*. Ipswich, MA: Gambit, 1982.

Morgan, Lewis Henry. *League of the Ho-de-no-sau-nee, or Iroquois* [1855]. New York: Corinth Books, 1962.

Siegel, Beatrice. *Fur Trappers and Traders*. New York: Walker & Co., 1981.

Tehanetorens [Ray Fadden]. *Tales of the Iroquois*. Rooseveltown, NY: *Akwesasne Notes*, 1976.

Wallace, Anthony F. C. *The Death and Rebirth of the Seneca*. New York: Random House, 1969.

Wallace, Paul A. W. *The White Roots of Peace*. Santa Fe, NM: Clear Light Publishers, 1994.

Wolfson, Evelyn. *The Iroquois: People of the Northeast*. Brookfield, CT: The Millbrook Press, 1992.

ISHI (1857–1914)

Ishi was the last known surviving member of the Yahi division of the Yana tribe of North American Indians. For years, he hid from white settlers in northern California. But in August 1911, at the age of fifty-four, he left the foothills of Mount Lassen and came forward to the town of Oroville in Butte County. Starving and grieving, he allowed himself to be captured. From that point forward, he was called *Ishi*, the Yahi word for "man."

The Hokan-speaking Yana Indians occupied the northeastern foothills of the Sacramento Valley in California. The Yahi division lived along Mill and Deer Creeks, which branched off the Sacramento River. They fished, hunted, and foraged for foods such as acorns. Their winter homes were earth-covered lodges, and in summer, they lived in thatched structures.

Massacred or driven from their homes by white miners during the 1860s, the Yana population dropped from nineteen hundred to thirty-five. The surviving Indians went into seclusion for forty years.

Throughout most of his life, Ishi was a member of a small band of the tribe that, at one time, numbered about a dozen. During the last few years prior to his coming forward, Ishi spent his days with just three people. They were probably his parents and sister. During the final months just before he arrived at Oroville, he was alone. He came forward because he was hungry, without weapons, and lonely. When found, his hair was still singed from his participation in a mourning ritual over the loss of his family.

Once discovered by the whites, Ishi was jailed for safekeeping. He spoke no English. The newspapers throughout the United States sensationalized him, calling him "the last wild Indian in North America."

After a few days in jail, Ishi was taken to San Francisco, where he was put in touch with noted anthropologists Alfred Kroeber and T. T. Waterman of the University of California's anthropology department. Ishi was housed in a museum at the University of California, where anthropologists could study him. Countless "tourists" visited the museum to see Ishi and to watch him make arrowheads. During that time, Ishi learned six hundred English words.

Because of their study of Ishi, scientists were able to gather a great deal of ethnographic and linguistic information about the Yana culture. Ishi showed them the ancient skills, including flint shaping and bow making. The anthropologists took him to his original home from time to time, where Ishi demonstrated his skills at making a salmon harpoon, snaring a deer, and shaping a bow from juniper wood.

Theodora Kroeber wrote the book *Ishi in Two Worlds*, and books about the Yahi language and culture were also published. Ishi survived just a few years after making contact with the outside world. He died of tuberculosis in 1914.

ISLETA PUEBLO

Isleta Pueblo is regarded as a southern pueblo in relation to the other pueblos of New Mexico. It is located 15 miles (24 kilometers) south of the city of Albuquerque. In its present location since before the arrival of the Spanish, Isleta Pueblo is composed of several communities along the Rio Grande. The pueblo has 211,103 acres (84,441 hectares) of land and a population of between three and four thousand.

The language of Isleta Pueblo is Tiwa, a branch of the Tanoan language. Other Tiwa-speaking Pueblos include Picurís, Sandia, and Taos. The Tanoan language has two other branches, Towa (spoken at Jemez Pueblo) and Tewa (spoken at Nambe, Pohoaque, San Ildefonso, San Juan, Santa Clara, and Tesuque Pueblos). For many centuries, Pueblo peoples have been multilingual, speaking the language of their own pueblo and quite frequently several languages or dialects of other pueblos.

With the colonization of New Mexico by the Spanish, Pueblo peoples gradually started becoming bilingual, tending to use only Spanish and the language of their own pueblo, rather than the languages of other pueblos. Today, the trend toward bilingualism is continuing, with English replacing Spanish as the second language.

Life became very difficult for all Pueblo people when the Spanish colonized New Mexico in 1598. After eight decades of mistreatment, which included forced labor and religious repression, the Pueblo people revolted. Some people of Isleta did not participate in the Pueblo Revolt of 1680, which drove the Spanish out of New Mexico for twelve years.

Isleta Pueblo potter Stella Teller. Pueblo pottery has been internationally appreciated since early in the twentieth century.

Those Isletas, fearing reprisals from the other pueblos that had participated in the revolt, fled southward with the Spanish and, along with some other Tiwa-speaking peoples, founded the pueblo of Ysleta, Texas, near El Paso. For the Pueblo people who remained in New Mexico, including most of the people of Isleta, the revolt proved to be an important event in improving their lives. Though the Spanish returned after a relatively short time, reforms were instituted, such as doing away with

A nativity scene crafted by Isleta Pueblo potter Stella Teller.

the encomienda system of forced labor, which made Pueblo-Spanish relations much better for the remainder of the Spanish colonial era.

By the terms of Article 8 of the Treaty of Guadalupe Hidalgo, which was signed on May 10, 1848, and ended the war between Mexico and the United States, all inhabitants, including the Pueblos, of the newly ceded territories automatically became citizens of the United States. This created confusion as to whether Pueblo people were still legally Indians. In 1876, a U.S. Supreme Court decision, *United States v. Joseph,* held that Pueblos were not legally Indians. Stripped of federal protection, the Pueblos suffered immediate encroachments on their lands. In 1913, the *Joseph* case was overturned by the U.S. Supreme Court, which allowed the Pueblos to gain access to federal programs. But that decision also brought them under religious persecution by the federal government. A series of regulations of the Bureau of Indian Affairs (BIA), known as the Religious Crimes Code, made it illegal for Native people to practice their traditional religions. Pueblos soon found their ceremonial objects confiscated and their religious leaders jailed.

Conditions improved when Congress passed the Pueblo Lands Bill on June 7, 1924, which forced the eviction of squatters from Pueblo lands and made compensation for other lost land. In 1947, a long-standing dispute between rival factions at Isleta was resolved by the adoption of a constitution for the pueblo. In 1970, the people of Isleta adopted another new constitution. Their form of government places much more of the power in the executive branch than most other tribal governments, with a governor having primary responsibility for the pueblo, along with a tribal council, whose members are appointed by members of the executive branch. All enrolled tribal members of Isleta who are twenty-one years old or older can vote in the election for governor, which occurs every two years. Tribal enrollment at Isleta requires one-half or more of Isletan blood.

Isletans have gained a wide reputation as skilled firefighters, and their firefighting teams are flown to major forest fires throughout the West. At home, many Isletans find employment in the city of Albuquerque, where they commute to work from the pueblo. Politically, their ongoing struggle is to protect their land and water rights, which requires constant vigilance. Toward that end, Isleta participates actively with the other pueblos of New Mexico in the All-Indian Pueblo Council.

— D. L. Birchfield

SEE ALSO:
All-Indian Pueblo Council; Bureau of Indian Affairs; Encomienda; Guadalupe Hidalgo, Treaty of; Pueblo; Pueblo Revolt of 1680; Spain.

ISPARHECHER (1829–1902)

Isparhecher (pronounced "spy-hee-cha"), was a full-blood, traditional Creek (Muscogee) leader who was elected principal chief of the Creek Nation in 1895. He had spent most of his life leading a large minority faction of Creek traditionalists in their attempts to dissolve the centralized Creek national government and return the nation to the traditional, decentralized system of town governments. But when the United States sought to force the allotment of Creek lands to individual tribal members, the Creeks turned to Isparhecher for leadership during the crisis. He died three years after his term of office ended while still attempting to stop the allotment of tribal lands by the Dawes Commission.

Isparhecher was born in 1829 in a village of the Lower Creeks of the Muscogee Confederation in Alabama. He was born into the tiger clan, the clan of his mother, Kecharte. His father was Tardeka Tustanugga. His parents were conservative, traditional Creeks, and their village was loyal to the William McIntosh faction of the confederation. Isparhecher was raised in the Creek traditions. He never learned English. He was still a child when he and his parents and the nations of the Muscogee Confederation were forced to remove from their homeland to Indian Territory. His parents either died on the Trail of Tears or died shortly after arriving in the West.

Isparhecher became a farmer, until the U.S. Civil War divided the Creek Nation. Isparhecher was also torn between the contending factions. At first, he followed the prevailing sentiment among the Creeks of the Lower Towns, who favored the South. He enlisted on August 17, 1861, in Company K of the Creek Mounted Volunteers of the Confederate Army. By 1863, he had become disillusioned with the Confederacy and switched his allegiance, enlisting on May 12 of that year in the Kansas Infantry Home Guards of the Union Army. He, along with many other Creeks who fought for the North, became identified as the "Loyal Creek faction."

After the war, he was elected to the legislature of the Creek Nation, and in 1872, he was elected a district judge. The Creeks adopted a new constitution after the Civil War, a centralized government patterned after the federal government of the United States. Many Creeks opposed this departure from their traditional, autonomous town governments. This traditional faction was led by Lochar Harjo. Isparhecher became an influential member of the traditional faction, and when Lochar Harjo died in the 1870s, Isparhecher became the leader of the faction, which consisted of about one-third of the Creek Nation.

This division within the nation became increasingly bitter and almost led to bloodshed in 1881 when armed supporters of both sides faced one another. By 1883, violence erupted when a dispute over election procedures could not be resolved. In that year, in what is known as the Green Peach War, Isparhecher led his people in an armed engagement against the Creek Militia, led by Pleasant Porter, which took place in an orchard of green peaches near the town of Okmulgee. In a series of skirmishes, Isparhecher and his followers were driven out of the Creek Nation and into the Cherokee Nation, where they found refuge. The United States Army intervened. In a settlement in which Isparhecher and his followers agreed to pledge allegiance to the Creek national government in return for new elections, they were allowed to return. Isparhecher won a narrow victory as principal chief in the election, but he resigned a few weeks later, declaring that the nation was too deeply divided for his leadership to be effective.

He continued to be a candidate for principal chief during the 1880s and 1890s, and he served for a time as chief justice of the Creek Nation. Finally, in 1895, he again won election as principal chief when a large majority of Creeks united behind his vigorous opposition to the allotment of tribal lands, which the U.S. Congress was in the process of forcing upon the Indian nations in Indian Territory by means of the Dawes Commission. During his four-year term, however, he was unable to oppose the power of the Congress. He died in 1902, still trying to stop the opening up of Creek lands to non-Native settlement.

— D. L. Birchfield

SEE ALSO:
Cherokee; Civil War, U.S., Indians in the; Creek; Dawes Commission; General Allotment Act; Oklahoma; Trail of Tears.

JACKSON, ANDREW (1767–1845)

Andrew Jackson was born in 1767 in South Carolina. As a young lawyer, he became wealthy by acquiring eighty thousand acres (thirty-two thousand hectares) of land recently taken from the Cherokees. He became a congressman and a senator from Tennessee, then a judge, and a major general of the Tennessee militia.

Jackson became famous, however, as an Indian fighter. It almost seems as if he knew that killing Indians was his path to fame. In 1813, in command of an army of eighteen hundred militiamen, he went into the Creek country of Alabama to attack the so-called Red Stick Creeks. Jackson received credit for a decisive victory at a place called Horseshoe Bend over the Red Sticks, a strongly traditional element of the Creek Nation. However, it should be pointed out that Jackson and his frontiersmen (Sam Houston and Davy Crockett were among them) did not go alone into this fight.

The Red Sticks were opposed within their own Creek Nation by the "progressive Creeks," who outnumbered them. Jackson's forces were heavily rein-

forced by these progressive Creeks—and by Cherokees and Choctaws—bringing his total force to around five thousand. Many analysts have maintained that it was Cherokee strategy and action that really saved the day for Jackson. It has even been said that Jackson's life was saved on the battlefield by a Cherokee named Junaluska.

Jackson's attitude toward Indians and Indian treaties is clearly illustrated by his treatment of the Creeks following his victory over the Red Sticks. It has been said that the United States government broke every treaty it ever made with an Indian tribe. That statement is not quite true.

The treaty that Jackson forced on the Creeks in 1814 is an example of what has been called a "victor's treaty." It was completely one-sided; it made demands on the Creeks but made no promises to them. Thus, there were no promises in the treaty to be broken later.

With this treaty, Jackson also took land away from the progressive Creeks, the very ones who had helped him win the victory over the Red Sticks. In the mind of Jackson, it seems, the real purpose of the war was to gain personal glory and to acquire land for the United States. Jackson took the most desirable land, not worrying about whose land it was.

When Jackson became president of the United States in 1829, the southern states, particularly Georgia, were already agitating for the removal of the Indian tribes from the Indian land that the states claimed. Jackson became their champion. The new president took out an old plan that had been devised by President Thomas Jefferson but had been waiting for someone ruthless enough to put it into effect. Jackson brushed it off and set it into motion.

The Indian policy of the Jackson administration became a policy of removal. He didn't worry about the rights of the Indians. Once, when someone mentioned that subject as set forth in treaties with the United States, Jackson replied that he had always viewed treaties with Indians as nothing more than an expediency. In other words, Jackson's attitude toward treaties made with Indian nations was to promise them anything that would get them to sign the treaty. The promise didn't really matter, for he had no intention of keeping it anyway.

With the issue of the removal of the Indians from the southern states, Jackson took two major

A nineteenth-century engraving depicts Chief Weatherford of the Creeks and General Andrew Jackson, after the Battle of Horseshoe Bend in March 1814.

approaches. First, he began pressuring Congress to pass an Indian Removal Bill that would mandate the removal of the tribes. Second, he refused to come to the aid of the tribes when the southern states, again especially Georgia, began harassing them. Eventually, his Removal Bill was passed into law, but the United States Supreme Court declared it to be unconstitutional. The president's reaction was typical of Jackson. "John Marshall has made his decision," he is reported to have said, in reference to the chief justice of the U.S. Supreme Court. "Let him enforce it."

To further expedite the process, Jackson sent a team of negotiators into the Indian country to coerce the Indians to sign removal treaties. One example will again serve to illustrate Jackson's methods. Under the leadership of Principal Chief John Ross, the Cherokee Nation refused to sign a treaty of removal, insisting instead upon its rights to its own Native land. Jackson's negotiators then, in 1835, concluded a treaty, the Treaty of New Echo-

ta, with individual Cherokees who were not authorized by the Cherokee Nation's government or people to do anything. In spite of its illegality, the treaty was ratified and ultimately enforced.

Jackson was replaced as president in 1837 and therefore did not preside over the completion of his nefarious plan. That chore was left to President Martin Van Buren.

In fact, the removal was never quite completed. Remnants of each of the southeastern tribes still remain in their old homelands. However, the vast majority of each tribe were removed, and that sad fact of United States history was largely due to the willingness of President Andrew Jackson to ignore the laws of his own country to accomplish his ends.

— R. J. Conley

SEE ALSO:
Cherokee; Creek; Five Civilized Tribes; Gold Rush; Junaluska; Removal Act, Indian; Ross, John.

Helen Hunt Jackson, author of *A Century of Dishonor*.

ans to the degree that Harriet Beecher Stowe's *Uncle Tom's Cabin* had done regarding Black slavery.

Despite her intentions as a reformer, Jackson's work was often used to support legislation harmful to Indians such as the Dawes Act (passed by Congress in 1887), which would divide many Native Americans' common landholdings among individuals. Such allotments often were sold to non-Indians, eroding Native American land bases, cultures, and languages. In the late 1800s, there were practically no non-Indian reformers who asserted a Native right to land, language, and culture. Instead, they sought, as some said, to "kill the Indian and save the man" as an alternative to outright extermination. Jackson's work played into the plans of reformers who, with the intention of "saving" Indians, supported assimilation and allotment.

SEE ALSO:
Dawes Commission; General Allotment Act.

JACKSON, HELEN HUNT
(1830–1885)

A wave of compassion for Native people was stirred by the publication of Helen Hunt Jackson's *Century of Dishonor* in 1881. Jackson, a friend of poet Emily Dickinson, also wrote a novel, *Ramona*, which put into a novelistic form the ravages of most Indian people's lives as described factually in *A Century of Dishonor*. The book went through three hundred printings and later inspired several movies. Jackson said at the time that she wanted *Ramona* to raise indignation regarding mistreatment of Indi-

JAMAICA

When Columbus first stopped in Jamaica (and claimed it for Spain) during his second voyage in 1504, the island was populated by Native peoples so numerous that the Spanish priest Bartolomé de Las Casas said Jamaica "abounded with Arawaks as an ant-hill with ants." Columbus described the Native peoples as generally friendly, although his first visit included a shower of arrows. The Arawaks also were nearly defenseless, no match for even a small party of armed Spaniards.

Columbus described the island as "dark and green" when his ships landed in the port that the English would later call St. Ann's Bay. A group of Native people met him: "One of the canoes was . . . large . . . and brightly painted. . . . [T]he chief came in person, with his wife and two daughters, of whom one was a very lovely girl of some eighteen years, entirely nude as they are wont to be, and very modest." The Arawaks met Columbus with a large party of canoes and ceremony: "Some had instruments on which they played; others had trumpets or conches [shells] elaborately decorated with birds and other devices. Others wore helmets or headdresses of green feathers arranged in a pattern." Columbus watched Arawaks make flour from sweet cassava and fashion it into tortillas. The tortillas were served with oysters and fish. Columbus soon sailed back to Cuba with one of the Arawaks on board. He returned to Jamaica again in 1503 on his fourth voyage.

Within just a few decades, Jamaica became one of several prizes in a maritime and mercantile contest between Spain, England, and France. Spanish colonization of Jamaica developed slowly. In the meantime, the Arawaks were dying of epidemic European diseases, including smallpox. In 1511, Las Casas visited Jamaica and was horrified by the number of dead and dying Indians. He returned to Spain and pleaded with King Ferdinand and Queen Isabella to help them. In 1611,

the Spanish abbot in residence counted 1,510 people living on the island, including only 74 Arawaks. While it is possible that the abbot did not count all of the Indians on the island, it was obvious that the great majority had died. By the time the English invaded the island and replaced the Spanish in 1655, not one pure-blooded Arawak was said to have survived.

Disease was a problem for Europeans as well as for Indians on Jamaica. The Spanish population never thrived, and many English colonists died of

A Native girl of mixed ancestry in Negril, Jamaica.

various tropical diseases. By 1700, nearly all the people on Jamaica were English-speaking descendants of Africans brought to the island as slaves on English plantations, many of which failed after their owners died or moved away. Today, Jamaica's population is primarily of African descent.

SEE ALSO:

Arawak; Columbus, Christopher; Las Casas, Bartolomé de; Spain.

JAMES BAY HYDRO-ELECTRIC PROJECT

On April 30, 1971, the James Bay Hydro-Electric Project was announced by Quebec provincial officials and the heads of several utility companies owned by the province. This announcement gave birth to a massive program for exploiting natural resources in the James Bay region of northern Quebec. The announcement also gave birth to a massive series of protests and court battles to preserve the environmental integrity of the James Bay region, long inhabited by various Native peoples who, even today, depend on it for their food and livelihood.

For years, utility companies had explored the hydroelectric potential of northern rivers in James Bay. With this new project, all major rivers flowing west into James Bay or north into Ungava Bay were to be dammed or diverted to produce electricity. Quebec, through Hydro-Quebec, would sell this electric power to Canadian and U.S. customers alike.

The James Bay Hydro-Electric Project was divided into three phases. In 1972, the Quebec government and Hydro-Quebec announced that the first phase would begin on the LaGrande River (Fort George River). The second phase would dam the Great Whale River and divert the Little Great Whale River into the larger river to increase its flow. The third phase, the NBR Project, would dam and divert the Nottaway, Ruperts, and Broadback Rivers.

The Cree and Inuit peoples have lived in the James Bay area for thousands of years. But Robert

The spillway and dam at LG-2 of the James Bay Hydro-Electric Project flooded the ancestral lands of the Chisasibi Crees in Quebec, Canada.

Bourassa, then premier of Quebec, and officials of Hydro-Quebec and the James Bay Energy Corporation refused to admit that the Crees and Inuit occupied this region. Neither the Crees nor the Inuit have signed treaties to cede their lands to any level of government. But, despite Cree protests to the contrary, Bourassa insisted that this land was uninhabited and that it was all right to flood the land. Exploitation of the LaGrande began—without consultation or negotiation with the Crees and Inuit.

The Crees and Inuit have always depended on the land for their survival. To this day, both nations pursue a lifestyle of hunting, gathering, and fishing. They see—and oppose—the hydroelectric project as a threat to their way of life.

The eight Cree communities (Chisasibi, Wemendji, Némiscau, Waskaganish, Whapamagoostui, Waswanapi, Eastmain, and Mistassini) formed a political union called the Grand Council of the Crees. Through this organization, the Crees began a series of court actions in an effort to stop the hydroelectric project. On November 15, 1972, the Crees and Inuit won a court injunction. Justice Malouf ordered the James Bay Development Corporation to stop construction and leave the territory. The Malouf judgment was later overturned by Justice Marcel Crete through the Quebec Appeal Court, and in April 1973, the Canadian Supreme Court refused to hear an appeal by the Crees regarding the Crete judgment.

Because construction in and around the Radisson community had already begun, the Quebec government persuaded the courts to allow the project to continue. The Crees had no choice but to negotiate and sign an agreement with the federal and provincial governments, an agreement that extinguished their claims and land rights to most of the region. The James Bay and Northern Quebec Agreement was ratified and signed on November 11, 1975.

The worst Cree fears about the destructive power of the project were realized with the completion of LG-2. Since its completion, the dam at LG-2 has flooded the ancestral burial grounds, fishing sites, and trap lines of the Chisasibi Crees. The level of mercury (a poisonous metal) of their main staple food, fish, has risen to dangerous levels, making it inedible. Migration routes of caribou and other large mammals, upon which the Crees depend for food and clothing, have been disrupted. Drinking water for the Eastmain Crees has been polluted. In view of this, the Crees launched a campaign to halt the final two phases of the James Bay Hydro-Electric Project.

After the victory of Parti Quebecois in the 1994 Quebec Province election, Premier Jacques Parizeau announced the postponement of the final two phases of the James Bay Hydro-Electric Project. For the Crees and Inuit, this signaled a major victory in their fight to halt the project that threatened to destroy their homeland and cultures. Environmentalists and other support groups in the United States have convinced states such as Massachusetts and New York to reconsider the energy deals they have signed with Quebec. Meanwhile, the struggle in Quebec to terminate the project continues.

— K. Wootton

SEE ALSO:

Akwesasne (St. Regis Reservation), Pollution of; Cree Indians and the James Bay II Project; Quebec.

JAMESTOWN

Jamestown was the first permanent English settlement in North America. On May 14, 1607, Captain Christopher Newport and 104 men claimed a strategic position on the James River in what is now the state of Virginia. This area was the home of an alliance of Algonquian tribes called the Powhatan Confederacy. The leader of this confederacy was Wahunsonacock; the English called him by the name of his confederacy, Powhatan. He ruled from his capital city, Werowocomoco.

The confederacy joined over two hundred villages and thirty tribes and could put hundreds of warriors into the field. Wahunsonacock's father had begun the confederacy, and Wahunsonacock added greatly to it during his lifetime. When the English first met him, he was over sixty years old.

Wahunsonacock could have easily wiped out the entire English settlement if he had chosen to do so. The English suffered greatly in the early years of the colony and were weak from hunger and disease. Of the first 900 colonists who came to

An early depiction of the arrival of Europeans at Jamestown.

Jamestown during its first three years, 750 died. Instead of growing crops, the colonists spent their time searching for gold, silver, and a northwest passage to India and China.

Captain John Smith helped the colony in many ways after he arrived in 1608. He traded with the Powhatans and did all he could to keep relations between the two groups friendly. Wahunsonacock had his men give the colonists corn, and they also traded at a rate of a bushel of corn for one square inch of copper. But the Indian leader eventually became convinced that the English were dangerous, and he captured Captain Smith, who was to be executed. Legend has it that Wahunsonacock's daughter saved the Englishman. Pocahontas, whose real name was Matowaka, would have been twelve at the time of the incident. Even if she didn't actually save Smith's life, Matowaka certainly played a large role in saving Jamestown by providing the colony with needed food.

In 1609, relations with the Indians worsened when a new governor came to Virginia—Sir Thomas Dale held Matowaka hostage. Around

thirteen years old, she was married to a warrior named Kocoum. While a prisoner, Matowaka/Pocahontas became a convert to Christianity and took the English name Rebecca. Around 1613 (some sources say 1614), she married John Rolfe, who was a successful farmer of Jamestown's new cash crop, tobacco. A son, named Thomas, was born to the couple in 1615. In 1616, the family journeyed to England, where Lady Rebecca Rolfe was a great public success and was even entertained by the royal family. In 1617, however, at the age of twenty-one, she contracted an illness and died.

It was tobacco that led to even more problems in terms of Indian-colonist relations. Huge profits could be made from growing tobacco and sassafras, which was believed at the time to cure syphilis, but clearing land to grow the crops was very difficult. It was much easier to attempt to gain Indian fields which already existed.

When Wahunsonacock died in 1618, his brother became the new leader. Opechancanough hated the English and planned for their complete removal. Between 1618 and 1622, he convinced members of the Powhatan Confederacy who were pro-English to join the anti-English group. In early 1622, an attack was launched, and 350 English colonists were killed in a matter of hours. In 1618, the total population of the English colony in Virginia was 350 people; if the attack had been launched in that year the English would have been wiped out. But in 1622, the English population was four times larger, and it vowed revenge.

For the next fourteen years, war raged between the English and the Indians. The English enjoyed their greatest single victory in 1625, when they wiped out and burned the town of the Pamunkey tribe and killed one thousand men, women, and children. In 1640, a peace agreement was made, and almost five years of peace followed. But in 1644, Opechancanough launched his second attack against the Jamestown colony. At the time of this attack, Opechancanough was said to be over one hundred years old. During the first two days of the new struggle, over five hundred colonists were killed, but English firepower turned the tide. Opechancanough was captured, and while a prisoner, he was shot by an English guard. With his death, Indian resistance to the Jamestown colony also ended.

But Jamestown continued to face problems. During Bacon's Rebellion (1676), in which a group of frontiersmen took over Jamestown in an effort to obtain reforms and promises of a bigger voice in the government of Virginia, Jamestown was burned to the ground. The town was rebuilt, but in 1699, Williamsburg became the state capital.

Jamestown's activities and population declined, and nature began to reclaim the land. By 1890, all that remained of the former settlement was the 1639 church tower. In 1893, the Association for the Preservation of Virginia Antiquities was formed, and the group gained the Jamestown site. The current fort and buildings that can be found at Jamestown are historical reproductions.

— T. Colonnese

SEE ALSO:

Algonquian; England; European Attitudes Toward Indigenous Peoples; Pocahontas; Virginia.

SUGGESTED READINGS:

Debo, Angie. *A History of the Indians of the United States*. Norman: University of Oklahoma Press, 1970.

Forbes, Jack D. *Columbus and Other Cannibals*. New York: Autonomedia, 1992.

Todorov, Tzvetan. *The Conquest of America*. Translated by Richard Howard. New York: Harper Collins 1984.

JEFFERSON, THOMAS (1743–1826)

Thomas Jefferson was president of the United States from 1801 to 1809. He was the first president to advocate the removal of eastern Indians to lands west of the Mississippi River. He drafted a constitutional amendment that would have authorized negotiation with Indian tribes for their lands in the East.

The amendment was never adopted. Instead, Indian removal was eventually carried out in the 1830s by act of Congress under the presidential administration of Andrew Jackson. Indian removal is so closely associated with Jackson that he is generally regarded as having originated the idea. But the idea was Jefferson's.

After Jefferson secured the Louisiana Purchase in 1803, he pressured eastern tribes to remove to this land in the West. The Choctaws were thought to be the eastern tribe most likely to agree to removal because of their history of friendly relations with Europeans and Americans. Great pressure was put on the Choctaw leaders at the negotiations for the treaty of Doak's Stand in 1805. The Choctaws, however, refused even to discuss the idea of removal. Jefferson's second term as president ended in 1809 without any eastern tribes having agreed to removal.

Jefferson's career had an impact on Indians in many other ways. He was the author of the Declaration of Independence, thereby playing an important role in the creation of the new land-hungry republic. As president, he authorized the expeditions of Lewis and Clark to the Pacific Northwest, which began the process of encroachment by the United States upon the lands of many western Indian nations.

SEE ALSO:

Choctaw; Declaration of Independence, U.S.; Jackson, Andrew; Removal Act, Indian.

JEWELRY, NATIVE AMERICAN

Like other kinds of jewelry, Native American jewelry grew out of the desire to create adornments for the body. And yet, there is much about Native jewelry that makes it different from the jewelry of other cultures. Earlier cultures, such as those of ancient Egypt and ancient Rome, regarded jewelry as symbols of wealth and rank, and the materials—gold, silver, and precious stones like diamonds and rubies—were more important than the designs. Native American people, on the other hand, did not have an economy based on precious metals like gold, and the jewelry they developed was based more on spiritual values and individual achievement. In most Native cultures, the value of jewelry lay in its ability to decorate and please the wearer and was thus very personal.

The earliest Native jewelry was made of a combination of bone, shell, hammered copper and silver, mica, and feathers. These materials were used to create patterns and forms ranging from necklaces to bracelets, earrings, and pendants. The forms were usually religious and represented personal spiritual beliefs.

Europeans who came to the Americas introduced materials and technologies that shaped later Native jewelry. The major colonial powers—the English, Dutch, French, and Spanish—brought and taught jewelry to Native craftspeople and created a desire for wealth among the people. Jewelry evolved then from spiritual expression in the form of bodily adornment to a more European symbol of status based on wealth or success. The acquisition of jewelry among Native people became important as a symbol within the tribe of the member's social rank and standing, a value that was based on Europeans standards.

The earliest jewelry that was introduced to Indian people by non-Natives was usually religious in nature, from silver crucifixes and Jesuit rings in the English or French Northeast to similar silver jewelry in the Spanish Southwest. Silver was the most popular material for making jewelry, whether it was engraved or embossed, and non-Native silversmiths used it to make gorgets (elaborate collars), earrings,

A deerskin dress decorated with shells and beadwork, from the Pacific Coast.

At a traditional clothing competition at the Santa Fe Indian Market in New Mexico, this Navajo girl displays a variety of jewelry, including finely crafted turquoise and silver pieces.

Navajo silver and turquoise jewelry. The Navajos have excelled at working with silver since learning the craft from a Mexican silversmith in the middle of the nineteenth century.

bands for headdresses, and brooches with elaborate cutout designs. These types of silver jewelry were called trade silver and were usually made by silversmiths in colonial communities for the growing fur trade industry in the expanding frontier. Gradually, Native people began working silver themselves, imitating the already-popular European pieces even as they began to include more Native spiritual symbolism. Certain European notions were taking hold, and a person with many rings, brooches, earrings, armbands, and bracelets was considered important within the community. Records of the day noted that the sister of the Mohawk leader Joseph Brant, Molly, had over six hundred silver brooches when she fled to Canada during the American Revolution.

Today, the common perception of Indian jewelry is that of the widely marketed Navajo and Zuni turquoise of the Southwest. Few people realize that these forms of jewelry emerged rather late in the nineteenth century, when the tribes of the Southwest adopted European silversmithing techniques to create an economy within their communities based on growing tourism to their regions. The use of turquoise, shell, and coral inlaid intricately in

silver has become the popular image of Native jewelry. This view fails to take into account the many other forms of jewelry—and materials used in jewelry—found among many tribes from Alaska to Florida. These include bone and horn chokers, beaded and quilled earrings, silver roach spreaders, and the rings, bracelets, armbands, and brooches that are still as fashionable and are produced in as great a number as they ever were.

While traditional forms like squash-blossom necklaces and conch (shell) belts of the Southwest are still popular, Native jewelry continues to grow and change. Today, the use of gemstones and mixed-metal elements (such as gold and platinum) have made Native jewelry a legitimate art form. And while antique Native jewelry continues to command high prices among collectors, the modern abstract pieces by prominent Native jewelers have created worldwide attention for a fine art form that has risen above the level of crafts.

— J. Monture

SEE ALSO:

Art and Design, Native; Brant, Joseph; Feathers and Featherwork; Navajo; Quillwork and Quillworkers; Zuni.

JEWS

Since the first Jewish settlers arrived in colonial America in 1654, Jewish-Americans have interacted with American Indians in a variety of ways. Those interactions have sometimes paralleled and sometimes contradicted the bloodied tradition of relations between Euro-Americans and Indians.

Most Jewish-Americans are descended from European Jews who did not arrive in the United States until after the massacre of Native people by U.S. troops at Wounded Knee in 1890. Even though Jews made up a mere fraction of 1 percent of the European population in colonial America, their arrival tested the supposed religious tolerance upon which colonial America had been founded. After running for their lives from oppressive governments in Spain, Portugal, and North Africa, and then living for a few generations in relative peace in Holland, the first Jews in the United States actually came from Brazil. They had settled there until the Portuguese invaded and drove them out. Some of these Jews returned to Amsterdam, others sailed for Curaçao and other ports in the West Indies, while still others, such as the Gomez family, arrived in New Amsterdam.

Restricted from many of the conventional occupations of the emerging colonial economy, Jewish settlers were among the first to seek out less conventional livelihoods, including trade with the Indians. The Gomez trading post, built in 1719 near Algonquian meeting grounds in New York State, still stands today. Like other early Jewish traders, Gomez would offer axes, decorative silks, silver charms, and whiskey for mink, muskrat, or sable pelts. This alliance between American Indians and pioneer Jews is responsible, in part, for the rise of some Jewish families, such as the Astors, to preeminence among American furriers.

Jewish history throughout the world is largely a story of surviving one persecution or massacre after another. Because this is so much a part of their history and identity, American Jews were among the first non-Indians to recognize the injustices committed against Indians by Euro-Americans. For example, Bernard Goldsmith, Moses Baruh, and Wolf Kalisher were among nineteenth-century American Jews who became friends with Indians and learned their languages and ways. These men also served as advisors and court interpreters, helping Indians argue for their rights in Courts of Indian Offenses. Kalisher befriended Manuel Olegario, a Temecula chief who had been deposed by a corrupt Indian Affairs agent. For more than a decade, Kalisher championed Olegario's cause, eventually helping him to get an audience with President Ulysses S. Grant, who reinstated Olegario as leader of his people. Today, this same sense of group identity and commitment to social justice has led the Simon Weisenthal Center and many local Jewish councils to oppose the use of school mascots, team logos, or nicknames that offend American Indians.

But for every Kalisher and Baruh, there was a Louis Kahn or an Arthur Morrison. Both of these men were self-proclaimed Indian fighters who joined with Kit Carson in his violent campaign against the Navajo.

To the astonishment of both Jew and Indian, Christian leaders throughout history have lumped the two peoples together, based not on their shared history of persecution but on the bizarre belief that American Indians are descended from the fabled lost tribes of Israel. This theory can be traced back to the questionable observations of friars who accompanied Spanish explorers in the early sixteenth century. These friars thought Indians resembled Jews because both had long noses and gutteral voices, lived in tribes, and built temples. They further believed that Indian languages bore eerie similarities to Hebrew.

In the 1650s, British clergyman Thomas Thorowgood used this theory to raise money to send missionaries to North America to convert the Indians to Christianity. In the early nineteenth century, Elias Boudinot, once president of the Continental Congress, proposed a plan to remove Indians from America and return them to their Jewish homeland. For a while, nineteenth-century social reformer Mordecai Manuel Noah invited Indians to join him and other American Jews in a utopian colony. However, no Indians and very few Jews took him up on his offer. Today, the notion of a utopian colony is generally dismissed as a far-fetched idea by all but a few, such as the Mormons, for whom it remains a viable part of their religious literature.

Between 1890 and 1920, 2.5 million Jews immigrated to the United States from Eastern Europe.

Most of them encountered new versions of the same barriers to acceptance that had greeted the Gomez family two hundred years earlier. Once again, out of economic necessity, Jews turned to unconventional occupations, including show business and popular culture. As a consequence, American Jews have had much influence, good and bad, on the portrayal of Indians in the media. Some Jewish portrayals of Natives include Chief White Halfoat in Joseph Heller's book *Catch–22* and Mel Brooks's movie spoof of the Old West, *Blazing Saddles*, in which a tiny group of African-American pioneers is befriended by a group of Indians who speak to each other in Yiddish (a gutteral-sounding language imported from the Jewish ghettos of Eastern Europe that bears a stronger resemblance to German, Hebrew, and Slavic strains than to any American Indian tongue).

Recently, an issue has risen between Jews and Indians over the use of the term *holocaust* to describe the history of Indians in post–European-contact America, in particular the massacres of Indians in California. For American Jews, the term *Holocaust*, with a capital H, is emotionally charged. It refers specifically to the extermination and murder of six million European Jews by the Nazis in a four-year span in the 1940s. Without wanting to diminish in any way the horrors of other acts of racial or ethnic violence, American Jews feel that the term *holocaust* has been used too casually and that it belongs specifically to Jewish history. Some Jews and historians, however, have acknowledged the more generic meaning of holocaust. They recognize that it has already been appropriated by other groups to refer to a variety of ethnic atrocities, including the massacre of American Indians. These Jews and historians have adopted instead the Hebrew word *Shoah* to name Hitler's unspeakable acts of genocide.

— D. P. Press

SEE ALSO:

California Indians; Carson, Kit; Courts of Indian Offenses; Mormons; Navajo; Wounded Knee (1890).

JICARILLA APACHE

The Jicarilla Apache Reservation consists of 750,000 acres (300,000 hectares) in north-central New Mexico. There are two divisions among the

These Jicarilla White Clan racers are preparing to enter the Stone Lake ceremonial relay race on the Jicarilla Apache reservation in New Mexico.

The White Clan procession at the Stone Lake ceremonial relay races, on the Jicarilla Apache reservation in New Mexico.

Jicarillas, the Olleros ("Mountain People") and the Llaneros ("Plains People"). *Jicarilla* is a Spanish word meaning "Little Basket."

Jicarillas were living on the high plains of what is now northeastern New Mexico and southwestern Colorado and adjacent areas along the front range of the Rocky Mountains when the Spanish began colonizing New Mexico in 1598. The Jicarillas and the Spanish enjoyed friendly relations, engaging in mutually beneficial trade. When the historic southward migration of the Comanches from Wyoming to the southern Plains began displacing the Jicarillas from their homeland, beginning about 1700 in far northeastern New Mexico, the Spanish attempted to come to their aid militarily. The Comanche migration, however, could not be halted, and the Jicarillas moved into the Rocky Mountains of northern New Mexico, where they continued their close and friendly association with the Spanish.

When the United States gained control of the region, the Jicarillas were able to remain on a reservation in northern New Mexico in the area where they had lived for more than two centuries since being displaced by the Comanches. In 1907, the reservation was enlarged with the addition of a large block of land to the south of the original section. After World War II, oil and gas was discovered on the southern portion of the reservation, which, by 1986, was producing annual income of twenty-five million dollars (which dropped to eleven million during the early 1990s recession).

In the 1920s, most Jicarillas were stockmen. Many lived on isolated ranches, until drought began making sheep raising unprofitable. By the end of the 1950s, 90 percent of the Jicarillas had moved to the vicinity of the agency town of Dulce.

Approximately 70 percent of the Jicarillas still practice the Apache religion. When the first Jicarilla tribal council was elected, following the reforms

A Jicarilla Apache woman holds a cottonwood tree branch, which she will wave to bless and cheer the runners at the Stone Lake ceremonial relay races, on the Jicarilla Apache reservation in New Mexico.

of the Indian Reorganization Act of 1934 (also known as the Indian New Deal), ten of its eighteen members were medicine men and five others were traditional leaders from chiefs' families.

In 1978, a survey found that at least one-half of the residents of the reservation still spoke Jicarilla, and one-third of the households used it regularly. Jicarilla children in the 1990s, however, prefer English, and few of the younger children are learning Jicarilla today. The director of the Jicarilla Education Department laments the direction these changes are taking regarding the language, but no plans are underway to force the children to learn Jicarilla. In 1959, the Jicarillas incorporated their school district with the surrounding Hispanic towns. Within thirty years, its school board included four Jicarilla members, including the editor of the tribal newspaper. In 1988, the Jicarilla school district was chosen New Mexico School District of the Year.

Jicarillas are demonstrating a new pride in traditional crafts. Basketry and pottery making, which had nearly died out during the 1950s, are now valued skills once again, being taught and learned with renewed vigor. Many Apaches say they are trying to take the best of both worlds, to try to survive in the dominant culture while still remaining Apache.

Apaches have suffered devastating health problems from the latter half of the nineteenth century throughout most of the twentieth century. Many of these problems are associated with malnutrition, poverty, and despair. They have suffered incredible rates of contagious diseases such as tuberculosis. Once tuberculosis was introduced among the Jicarillas, it spread at an alarming rate. The establishment of schools, beginning in 1903, only gave tuberculosis bacteria a means of spreading rapidly throughout the entire tribe. By 1914, 90 percent of the Jicarillas suffered from tuberculosis, and between 1900 and 1920, one-quarter of the people died. One of the reservation schools had to be converted into a tuberculosis sanitarium in an attempt to address the crisis. The sanitarium was not closed until 1940.

Under the Indian Claims Commission Act of 1946, the Jicarillas have been awarded nearly ten million dollars in compensation for land unjustly taken from them, but the United States refuses to negotiate the return of any of this land. In *Merrion v. Jicarilla Apache Tribe*, the United States Supreme Court ruled in favor of the Jicarillas in an important case concerning issues of tribal sovereignty, holding that the Jicarillas have the right to impose tribal taxes upon minerals extracted from their lands.

Today, the Jicarilla Apaches operate a ski enterprise, offering equipment rentals and trails for a cross-country ski program during the winter months. The gift shop at the Jicarilla museum in Dulce, New Mexico, provides an outlet for the sale of locally crafted Jicarilla traditional items, including basketry, beadwork, feather work, and finely tanned buckskin leather. Tourism, especially for events such as tribal fairs and for hunting and fishing, provides jobs and brings money into the local economy. Deer and elk hunting is especially popular on the Jicarilla reservation. Permits are sold by the Jicarilla Game and Fish Department in Dulce. The Jicarillas maintain five campgrounds where camping is available for a fee. They host the Little Beaver Rodeo and Powwow, usually in late July, and the Gojiiya Feast Day on September 14 and 15 each year at Dulce, New Mexico.

— D. L. Birchfield

SEE ALSO:
Apache; Comanche; Indian Claims Commission Act; Indian New Deal (Indian Reorganization Act); New Mexico.

JOE, RITA (1932–)

Rita Joe, a Micmac poet, has been one of the most influential Native poets in Canada in the last quarter of the twentieth century. She was born in 1932 in Wycocomagh, Cape Breton Island, Nova Scotia, on the Eskasoni Reserve of the Micmac people. Her parents were Bernard and Annie Googoo. When she was five years old, her mother died in childbirth. She and her brothers and sisters were then raised by foster families in the Micmac community.

She attended Shubbenacadie Residential School until the eighth grade and then moved to the United States. In Boston, Massachusetts, she met and married her husband, a Micmac named Frank Joe. They soon had a large family, which included children of their own, others they had adopted, and others for whom they provided foster care. They moved back to the Eskasoni Reserve of the Micmac people on Cape Breton Island, where Frank Joe died in 1990.

During the 1960s, she wrote a column for the *Micmac News* entitled "Here and There in Eskasoni," and she began writing poetry. Much of her early poetry recalls her longing for her mother when she was a child, after her mother's death. She also found that she had a voice for decrying the marginalization of Canadian Native people in mainstream Canadian history and culture and in calling attention to the survival and experiences of contemporary Native people in Canada. Her first book, *Poems of Rita Joe* (Abenaki Press), gained wide attention when it was published in 1974. It won the poetry competition prize of the Nova Scotia Writers' Federation. Soon she was invited to speak to audiences all across the continent at libraries, schools, community centers, and universities. One of her poems was selected for display, printed on tanned hide, by the Canadian Museum of Civilization in Ottawa.

Her poetry began appearing widely in literary quarterlies and journals, and in 1988 she published her second volume of poems, entitled *Song of Eskasoni* (Ragweed Press). In recognition of the voice she has given, through her poetry, to the contemporary Native people of Canada, in April of 1990, in a ceremony in Rideau Hall in Ottawa, the Governor General of Canada bestowed upon her the highest honor that Canada can give to one of its citizens, the Order of Canada.

SEE ALSO:
Micmac.

JOHNSON, E. PAULINE
(1861–1913)

Emily Pauline Johnson was born in 1861, the youngest child of George Henry Martin Johnson, a Mohawk chieftain, and Emily Susanna Howells, daughter of a British Quaker family. She was raised at Chiefswood, the family manor near Brantford, British Columbia. She was schooled at home, and after two years of college, she took up a life of leisure at Chiefswood, entertaining her father's visitors and writing verse. Johnson was also influenced by her grandfather, Smoke Johnson, who told her traditional stories and filled her with a deep respect for her people.

Upon her father's sudden death, after outlaws beat him for opposing bootleg liquor on the reserve, the family could not afford to live in Chiefswood. Pauline Johnson and her mother moved into a small apartment nearby, and Johnson was confronted with the problem of earning a living. One January evening in 1892, she was invited to recite one of her poems at a Toronto literary evening. Johnson's reading was wildly popular, and first an entire evening, then a series of evenings, then a tour were arranged for her to read her verse across the country. This was the beginning of a performing arts career, which, along with her writing, supported her financially.

Johnson spent the 1894 season in London, where her first book of verse, *The White Wampum*, was accepted for publication. She returned to Canada to tour the country again and proceeded to cross the Rocky Mountains nineteen times, visiting hundreds of cities and towns.

Johnson always performed for half the evening in Native garb, then changed into an evening gown for the remainder of her recital. She used the popular fascination with her image as the "Mohawk Princess" to educate and entertain her audiences. Her material, all original, counteracted prevailing stereotypes of Indians and highlighted the negative impact of Christianity and European culture on Canada's Natives. In addition to performing, Johnson continued to write both poetry and short stories for magazine publication, signing herself "Tekahionwake," her grandfather's name.

Near death in 1912, she had collected poetry published as *Flint and Feather* to assist in paying her doctor bills. The following year, *The Shagganappi* and *The Moccasin Maker* were published posthumously. Pauline Johnson was a well-known public figure when she died penniless of breast cancer in Vancouver, British Columbia, in 1913.

JOHNSON, WILLIAM (1715–1774)

Sir William Johnson was probably the most influential single Englishman with the Iroquois and their allies during the French and Indian War. From his mansion near Albany, Johnson forayed in Indian war parties, painting himself like an Indian, and taking part in ceremonial dances. Joseph Brant (also known as Thayendanegea), the Mohawk leader, fought beside Johnson at the age of thirteen, and Johnson was a close friend of the elderly Tiyanoga, with whom he traveled as a warrior. Tiyanoga, called Hendrick by the British, was a major figure in colonial affairs who visited England, allied himself with the British against the French, and advised Benjamin Franklin on the Iroquois form of government. Hendrick was killed making war on the French with Johnson at Lake George in 1755. Because he successfully recruited a sizable number of Iroquois to the British interest, Johnson was made a baronet, Sir William Johnson, with a monetary award of five thousand pounds sterling.

William Johnson learned the customs and language of the Mohawks and was well liked by the tribespeople. He had a number of children by Mohawk women and acknowledged them as such. He had several children by Mary Brant, a Mohawk clan mother and granddaughter of Hendrick. Hendrick had a high regard for the Englishman and expressed his regard when he said, ". . . he has Large Ears and heareth a great deal, and what he hears he tells us; he also has Large Eyes and sees a great way, and conceals nothing from us."

In June 1760, in the final thrust to defeat the French in North America, Johnson called for men to attack Montreal. About six hundred warriors responded along with many of the tribesmen living in the Montreal area. Sir William reported he was sending gifts to "foreign Indians" who were switching their allegiance from the French.

The defeat of the French and their departure

from Canada at the end of the war upset the balance that the Iroquois had sought to maintain between the British and the French. Reluctantly, they attached themselves to the British, but they could no longer play one European power against another. The English now occupied all the forts surrounding Iroquois country. Johnson played a key role in pressing the English crown to limit immigration west of the Appalachians, but land-hungry colonizers ignored royal edicts, intensifying conflicts over land. In the meantime, Johnson became one of the richest men in the colonies through land transactions and trade with Indians.

In his later years, Johnson agonized over whether to side with the British crown or the revolutionary patriots. The aging Sir William died at a meeting with the Iroquois on July 11, 1774, at his mansion near Albany. For two hours, Johnson had addressed the Iroquois in the oratorical style he had learned from them, summoning them to the British cause in the coming revolution of the English colonies. Suddenly, Johnson collapsed. He was carried to bed, where he died two hours later. The assembly of chiefs was stunned by his sudden death, but Guy Johnson, Sir William's nephew and son-in-law, stepped in to fill the breach left by his elder.

SEE ALSO:
Brant, Joseph; Canada, Native–Non-Native Relations in; Hendrick; French and Indian War; Iroquois Confederacy; Mohawk.

JOHNSON-O'MALLEY ACT

The Johnson-O'Malley Act, passed by Congress in 1934, authorized the Bureau of Indian Affairs to enter into contracts with state and local agencies for a variety of services for Indian people.

The best-known contracts for services to Native American people have dealt with the education of Native children. The federal government provides Johnson-O'Malley (JOM) funding to schools with Indian students. In most cases, the Indian

Sir William Johnson, an influential Englishman among the Iroquois in eighteenth-century colonial America.

nations themselves administer the program's funding, so the types of programs available vary from school to school. The first education contracts, which were made with state education departments, helped increase the attendance of Indian children in public schools. Taking Indian children from their families and communities and shipping them off to boarding schools, where they received training that minimized their identity as Indians and encouraged their assimilation into the dominant culture, had been the prevailing education policy of the U.S. government since the earliest days of the republic. Thanks to Johnson-O'Malley, however, within the first two years of these programs, enrollment by Indian children in boarding schools dropped by about ten thousand.

Also under the auspices of Johnson-O'Malley, the Bureau of Indian Affairs (BIA) hired ethnologists and historians to produce textbooks on Indian history and achievement to be used in its schools. It also hired linguists to help teach bilingual students who were less familiar with English. These experts helped not only in communicating lessons to Indian children in the classroom but in actually teaching them English, as well. In many cases, JOM funds allow schools to hire Indian educators who understand the students' backgrounds and help motivate them.

In some schools, Johnson-O'Malley provides needed tutoring for Indian students in a variety of subjects. JOM funds also help provide students with supplies at the beginning of the year and allow students to participate in extracurricular activities by helping them pay for sports clothing, yearbooks, and other supplies. Other educational tools provided through JOM funding include computers, textbooks, and other items needed to educate students and prepare them for the competitive world awaiting them when they graduate. JOM has also encouraged Native students to produce crafts by hiring experts to help market the crafts outside of school.

JOM also helps finance and set up cultural programs for Indian children. This service is especially valuable to nonreservation Indian children and Indian children living in cities, offering them classes in Native arts and crafts, literature, and even Indian languages that might otherwise not be available to them off of reservations.

Schools that are eligible to participate in the Johnson-O'Malley program must keep records of the number of students who are Indian and therefore eligible for JOM services. When these records are turned over to the BIA, the schools get a certain amount of money per Indian child. Thus Johnson-O'Malley is of value not only to Indian students but to public schools as well.

SEE ALSO:
Boarding Schools; Bureau of Indian Affairs.

JOHNSTON, BASIL H. (1929–)

Basil H. Johnston is a noted Ojibwe (Chippewa) author and linguist. He was born on July 13, 1929, on Parry Island Reserve, Ontario, Canada, the son of Rufus and Mary Johnston. Until the age of ten, he attended Cape Croker Indian Reserve School and then was sent to a school that was run by Jesuit priests.

In 1950, Johnston graduated valedictorian from that school, Garnier Residential School for Indian Boys, after having dropped out of school in the ninth grade and having worked at a number of jobs, including fishing, hunting, and trapping. In 1954, he received a B.A. degree from Loyola College in Montreal, and in 1962, he received a secondary school teaching certificate from the Ontario College of Education.

From 1957 to 1959, Johnston served as assistant manager, and from 1959 to 1961 as manager, of the Toronto Board of Trade. From 1962 to 1969, he was a teacher at Earl Haig Secondary School. Since 1969, he has been a lecturer in the ethnology department of the Royal Ontario Museum, and since 1974, he has also been a private language teacher for Ojibwe people.

Johnston's work and writings have brought him wide recognition and many awards, including the 1967 Centennial Medal in recognition of his work on behalf of Native peoples in Canada. In 1976, he received the Samuel S. Fells Literary Award for his essay "Zhowmin and Mandamin." In 1989, he received the Order of Ontario for service of greatest distinction and of singular excellence benefiting society in Ontario and elsewhere.

In one of Johnston's most recent books, *Indian School Days* (University of Oklahoma Press, 1989), he tells the story of his early life and the factors that led him to decide to return to school. He began publishing in 1970, with an essay entitled "Bread Before Books or Books Before Bread," which appeared in an anthology entitled *The Only Good Indian: Essays by Canadian Indians*. In that essay, he discusses the reasons for the deterioration of Indian traditional life. His essays regarding educational issues soon began appearing in Canadian magazines, including such titles as "Indian History Must Be Taught," in the March 1971 issue of *The Educational Courier*, and "Forget Totem Poles," in the March 1975 issue of the same publication.

In 1978, Johnston began publishing linguistic materials, including *Ojibway Language: Course Outline* and *Ojibway Language Lexicon for Beginners* (both published by the Ministry of Indian and Northern Affairs in Ottawa). In 1979, he published a novel entitled *Moose Meat and Wild Rice* (reprinted in 1993 by the University of Nebraska Press). He has published many other works, including *How the Birds Got Their Colours* (1978), *Tales the Elders Told: Ojibway Legends* (1981), *Ojibway Ceremonies* (1982), and *By Canoe and Moccasin: Some Native Place Names of the Great Lakes* (1986). In 1992, he helped conduct one of the workshops at Returning the Gift: A Festival of North American Native Writers at the University of Oklahoma, where the Native Writers' Circle of the Americas was founded.

SEE ALSO:
Returning the Gift.

JOINT USE AREA

By an act of Congress in 1958, Public Law 85-547, the U.S. government declared that the rights of Hopis and Navajos to the same parcel of land in northeastern Arizona would be decided in federal district court by a special panel of judges. This land consisted of a rectangle that surrounded the Hopi villages and lay completely within the Navajo Nation.

The rectangular parcel of land in question had been created by an ambiguous executive order in 1882. Accordingly, following the act of Congress in 1958, in 1962 a decision was rendered, known as *Healing v. Jones*, that decreed that both tribes held "joint, undivided and equal rights and interests" in a majority of the land in the rectangle. A smaller portion of the rectangle, known as District Six, was awarded to the exclusive use of the Hopis by the decision.

This decision established what became known as the Joint Use Area. The land within the rectangle lies mostly to the north of the Hopi villages, with small portions on the east, west, and south. Approximately one hundred Hopis and approximately five thousand Navajos were living within the rectangle at the time of the decision.

The Joint Use Area existed until 1974, when another act of Congress declared that a federal district court would partition the land into exclusive Navajo and Hopi sections. Accordingly, in 1977, a court decision divided the Joint Use Area between the two tribes, and all Navajos and Hopis who were found to be living on the wrong side of the boundary were ordered to move. Since this decision affected many more Navajos than Hopis, it has become a matter of great controversy within the Navajo Nation and has become the focus of attention nationally.

From its beginning in 1882, the rectangular area has been a source of confusion for everyone involved. The executive order that established it was brief. It set forth the boundaries of the rectangle—which extends about 70 miles (113 kilometers) north to south and about 56 miles (90 kilometers) east to west—and withdrew the land from the public domain, which made any non-Indian settlement on it illegal. It also stated that the land was "for the Moqui [Hopis] and such other Indians as the Secretary of Interior may see fit to settle thereon."

Researchers have found evidence that the executive order was not issued for the benefit of either the Hopis or the Navajos, but that it seems to have been the result of an Indian agent who was determined to find a way to remove from the Hopi villages two non-Indians who had challenged his authority. The commissioner of Indian Affairs did not require an investigation of the effects of the order upon the inhabitants of the area, and the order was not based on any examination of

The graffiti on this billboard, Relocation Is Genocide, expresses the sentiments of many people who support the efforts of the Navajo families who wish to remain on their land in the Navajo-Hopi Joint Use Area.

the Hopis' or the Navajos' needs. In fact, a number of field studies that addressed these needs were ignored when the order was announced.

During the 1930s, land management districts were created for the administration of federal programs in the area, and most of the land that the Hopis resided on was organized into a 630,000-acre (252,000-hectare) tract known as District Six. This included a portion of the rectangular area in the 1882 executive order. It was this District Six land that was awarded exclusively to the Hopis by the district court in the 1962 case of *Healing v. Jones*, which established the joint use area for the remainder of the rectangle. Though the Congress in 1974 ordered the joint use land partitioned between the two tribes, the case has continued to be one of great controversy throughout Indian country, mainly because the many Navajo families who are required to move by the court decision have been living on the land for generations.

SEE ALSO:
Hopi; Hopi and Navajo Relocation Act; Navajo; Navajo Reservation.

JONES, PETER (1802–1856)

Peter Jones was a Canadian Ojibwe (Chippewa) author, linguist, and religious leader who came to be regarded as the principal chief of the Missisauga Ojibwes. Also known as Kahkewaguonaby or Kahkewagonnaby, he was born on January 1, 1802, at Burlington Heights, Ontario, on the western shore of Lake Ontario. His mother was Tuhbenahneeguay, the daughter of Missisauga chief Wahbanosay. His father, a Welshman named Augustus Jones, was a government surveyor and a close friend of Mohawk leader Joseph Brant.

Peter Jones was raised as a traditional Ojibwe until the age of sixteen, when his father had him baptized as an Episcopalian. Thereafter, he entered into religious studies. In 1823, he joined his brother John in changing to the Wesleyan Methodist religion, and in 1830, he was ordained a minister in the Wesleyan Conference. He soon began producing translations of religious texts and hymns into the Ojibwe language.

In addition to his religious activities, he was also a political leader of the Missisaugas, and in this dual role he lobbied on behalf of the land rights of his people. He traveled extensively, making many trips to Toronto, New York, London, and other large cities. He married an English woman, and together they raised a large family.

His literary activities produced works of lasting value, among them one of the most important and enduring sources of information about his people, *A History of the Ojebway Indians*, published in 1861. Another important contribution, *The Life and Journals of Kah-ke-wa-quo-nā-by*, was published in 1860.

His constant travel and his habit of working to the point of exhaustion eventually broke his health while he was still a relatively young man. He died on June 29, 1856, at Brantford in Ontario. The next year, the Ojibwe people in Canada erected a monument to his memory.

One of his sons, who was also named Peter, followed his father's literary inclinations. He became editor and publisher of *The Indian*, an Ontario periodical devoted to the discussion of Indian issues.

SEE ALSO:
Brant, Joseph.

JONES, WILLIAM (1871–1909)

William Jones, a Mesquakie who was also known as Megasiawa or "Black Eagle," was an author and anthropologist who made major contributions to the field. Born on March 28, 1871, on the Sac and Fox Reservation in Indian Territory (present-day Oklahoma), Jones was the son of Sarah Penny, an Englishwoman, and Henry Clay Jones, of Welsh and Fox (Mesquakie) descent. When he was about a year old, Jones's mother died, and he was placed in the care of his Mesquakie grandmother. She cared for him until her death nine years later, teaching him the language and culture of their people.

At the age of ten, Jones entered an Indian boarding school run by the Society of Friends in Wabash, Indiana. After three years of schooling, he returned to his father's home in Indian Territory and worked as a cowboy. In 1889, Jones was recruited to attend the Hampton Normal and Agri-

In 1880, mostly because of military pressure from the Mexican army, Juh and his followers agreed to move to San Carlos. However, the next year, in August 1881, the United States Army, in attempting to suppress an Apache religious movement at San Carlos, precipitated violence at Cibecue Creek, and Juh, Geronimo, and many Apaches fled south to the mountains of northern Mexico.

In April of 1882, Juh executed a daring and spectacular military operation when his forces attacked San Carlos and freed hundreds of Membreno Apaches. Hotly pursued by several different units of the United States Army, Juh's forces fought three rear-guard engagements that allowed the Apaches to escape into the mountains of Mexico, though a number of them, mostly women and children, were killed by the Mexican army while Juh's fighting men were engaged against the Americans.

In November of 1883, Juh drowned after falling from his horse into water, possibly after suffering a heart attack. Geronimo succeeded to the leadership of the Chiricahuas and other Apaches who had followed Juh.

SEE ALSO:
Apache; Cochise; Geronimo.

JUNALUSKA (?–c. 1836)

Junaluska was a prominent Cherokee during the war with the Red Stick Creeks and again during the years just before the forced removal of the Cherokee Nation from its ancient homelands to present-day Oklahoma (then Indian Territory). In 1813, when he went with other Cherokees to join Andrew Jackson in his campaign against the Red Sticks, he was not yet known as Junaluska. He was called Gul kala ski, a name that has been roughly translated as "Something That Is Falling."

At the Battle of Horseshoe Bend, the bloody and decisive final battle of the Red Stick War, it has been said that Andrew Jackson had fallen on the field and was about to be killed by a Creek warrior. Gul kala ski stepped in and fought with the Creek, killed him, and thereby saved the life of Jackson. Jackson then, the story goes, swore eternal friendship not only to Gul kala ski, but to the Cherokees.

Some years later, in the troubled times just preceding the removal, with Andrew Jackson in the White House, Gul kala ski told his friends that he would go to Washington to see the president. Recalling Jackson's grateful pledge following the Battle of Horseshoe Bed, Gul kala ski was sure that Jackson would come to the aid of the Cherokees.

He made the trip and had himself announced, but to his chagrin, Jackson would not even give him an audience. Humiliated in front of his friends and disappointed in the man he had thought to be his friend, Gul kala ski said, "Detsinu lahungu," or "I tried but I failed." Thereafter, he was known as "Tsunalahunski," meaning, "he tried but failed." The name has been Anglicized as "Junaluska."

Junaluska died in the old Cherokee country just before the Trail of Tears. His descendants adopted his latest name in its anglicized version as a surname.

SEE ALSO:
Cherokee; Creek; Jackson, Andrew; Junaluska, Arthur Smith; Oklahoma; Removal Act, Indian; Trail of Tears.

JUNALUSKA, ARTHUR SMITH (1918–)

Arthur Junaluska, a Cherokee playwright, choreographer, director, producer, and lecturer, was born on November 30, 1918, in Cherokee, North Carolina. A descendant of prominent Cherokee leaders, including Junaluska and Yonaguska, he gave up a career in medical research for a career in the theater, where he has written many plays which explore Indian cultural values and which have been performed on radio, television, and the stage.

He was educated at Cherokee Indian School, Okmulgee Junior College, Maryville College, Western Carolina Teachers College, and the London School of Medicine. He engaged in medical research in England, and he is credited with modifying a blood test that is now used by commercial blood banks. However, while still in England, his love of theater led him to become the first American Indian to perform in a Shakespearean Repertory Company.

He returned to the United States after serving in the U.S. Army in World War II. In 1956, he organized the American Indian Dance Company to present Native American performing arts in the professional theater. For these productions, including *Dance of the Twelve Moons*, which he wrote and produced, he used only American Indian performing artists. In 1958, he served as director of drama at South Dakota Wesleyan University. Since then, he has served as executive and artistic director of the American Indian Society of Creative Arts.

In 1960–1961, he also served as director and coordinator of the Indian Village at Freedomland, an amusement park in New York City, where he worked with Native performing artists in presentations of tribal dances and songs. He has also served as director of performing arts at the Indian Festival of Arts in Oregon, and he has served as a consultant and technical advisor for movies and plays. He has also produced and directed plays unrelated to Indians, including one which is an evening with Edgar Allan Poe. An actor himself, and a member of Actors Equity and the Screen Actors Guild, he has appeared in many dramatic roles on radio and television, in the theater, and in movies.

Junaluska is the author of many productions, including *The Medicine Woman* (a drama), *The Spirit of Wallowa* (a drama), *Spectre in the Forest* (a drama), *The Man in Black* (a drama), *Shackled* (a documentary), *Hell-Cat of the Plains* (a drama), and *Grand Council of the Indian Circle* (a drama-pageant).

SEE ALSO:
Junaluska.

JUNEAU, JOSETTE (1803–1855)

Josette Juneau, a Menominee, was an influential figure in the early history of the city of Milwaukee,

Milwaukee in 1849, around the time when Josette Juneau, who was married to a prominent Euro-American business and political leader, chose to devote her time to living with and caring for fellow Native people.

Wisconsin, as that area was changing from one populated mostly by Indians to one populated mostly by non-Indians. She was a linguist who was fluent in Menominee, Chippewa, Potawatomi, Winnebago, French, and English. Her Menominee relatives included such influential leaders as Ahkanepoway and Onaugesa.

She was born in Sheboygan, Wisconsin, in 1803, one of twelve children of a Menominee woman and a French Canadian fur trader. She was educated in Catholic schools, and while still in her teens, she assisted in the education of younger students at St. Francis Xavier Mission near Green Bay, Wisconsin.

Josette Juneau, a Menominee, personally intervened to prevent violence between Native people and early residents of the Milwaukee area.

When she was seventeen years old, she married a French Canadian man, Soloman L. Juneau, who worked for her father at his trading outpost in Milwaukee. Her husband soon developed extensive business interests of his own and served as the first mayor of Milwaukee. As the wife of an influential businessman and civic leader, she might have become prominent in the social life of the rapidly growing town, but instead, she devoted her energies to providing extended nursing care for the ill and to assisting with other charities. For this work, she was acknowledged by a gift from Pope Leo XII.

Throughout her life, she preferred the company of the Native people of the region, refusing to mix socially with the ever-increasing number of Anglo-Americans and rarely speaking English. In 1853, her ties within the Native communities and her devotion to peace are credited with averting hostilities. In that year a group of Anglo-American squatters constructed a settlement on local Potawatomi lands that caused the Potawatomis to plan an attack on the settlement that would destroy it. Learning of the plan, and with her husband out of town, she took it upon herself to try to avert a crisis that she knew would only result in great harm to the Potawatomis. She maintained an all-night vigil in the settlement, which discouraged the Potawatomis from launching their plan, thereby averting hostilities.

To be closer to her Menominee relatives, she prevailed upon her husband to build a second home in the village of Theresa, Wisconsin, north of Milwaukee and close to the Menominee Reservation. This house was used for their summer home and as their retirement home after 1852. She died in Milwaukee in 1855 while undergoing treatment for an illness. Upon her death, she was eulogized in the local press.

Josette Juneau had eighteen children, fourteen of whom survived infancy. One of them, Joseph Juneau, traveled to Alaska, where he became a cofounder of the town of Juneau. In 1880, Joseph Juneau and four other men discovered gold at the site of the future town, starting a gold rush. In 1900 the town of Juneau, Alaska was incorporated, and in 1959, when Alaska became a state, Juneau became the state capital.

SEE ALSO:
Menominee; Potawatomi.

KACHINA

The Pueblo Indians—the Hopis, Zunis, and Rio Grande Pueblos—of present-day Arizona and New Mexico honor spirit beings or spirit powers called kachinas (katzinas). Kachinas have been participants in Pueblo religious ceremonies since pre–European-contact times, and early pottery and

A Hopi kachina, on display at the Museum of Northern Arizona.

This Hopi kachina doll belonged to a two-year-old Hopi girl.

According to Hopi belief, kachina spirits live on the tops of great mountains. Hopis believe that the kachina spirits reside half of each year with the living on the Hopi mesas and the other half on the mountaintops.

Masked dancers take part in Hopi kachina ceremonies from the winter solstice in late December to Niman (Home Dance) in July. The dances in this time period include Pamuya (Kiva Dances) in January, the Powamu (Bean Dance) in February, the Anktioni (Repeat Dances) in March, and the Soyohim (Plaza Dances) in April and May. The purpose of the Niman Dance in July is to say farewell to the masked dancers; to honor the ripening of crops, particularly corn; and for gift giving, such as the giving of carved dolls to young girls. Flat kachina dolls are given to infants to protect them. During Niman, cornmeal is tossed onto the kachina dancers, and prayers and gratitude are offered.

Hopi ceremonies also take place from July to mid-December during the time when kachinas are believed to return to the mountaintops. However, the dancers during this time period are unmasked.

Customs, legends, and traditional beliefs are all a part of the kachina representations. For instance, when young Hopi women are ready for marriage, their hair is placed on the sides of the head in two large circles. The Warrior Maiden kachina, however, has the hair on only one side of her head done in this large circle. Legend has it that as the woman was fixing her hair, she was interrupted by an enemy.

wall paintings contain images of masked kachina figures.

In religious ceremonies, the kachina spirits are represented by dancers wearing masks and regalia. The ceremonies take place during times dictated by the positions of the sun and moon in relation to established points on the horizon such as mountain peaks or mesa edges. They are performed with hopes of preserving harmony in the universe and good weather, particularly rain, for crops. Ceremonies are also performed to bring happiness, health, and longevity to the Pueblo people.

Wilford Duwyenie, a Hopi kachina carver, at work in Kykotsmovi, Arizona.

She immediately went into battle against the enemy with the hair on one side of her head hanging straight.

Kachina dolls are carved from cottonwood root and other materials in the form of various kachina spirits. Modern kachina doll carving combines tradition with contemporary creative methods and materials. Traditionally, the dolls were carved in one piece; more often today, largely because of the commercial sales of these dolls, the various parts of the doll are carved separately and then joined. After assembly, the doll is first whitewashed and then painted. The type of body paint often typifies a specific kachina. The painting of the mask is very detailed. Objects such as rattles, bows, whips, swords, knives, and sticks are placed in the hands. These objects are an important part of the kachina's identity. Jewelry, beads, shells, feathers, and colorful clothing further embellish the dolls, giving them special and individual meaning.

SEE ALSO:
Hopi; Pueblo; Zuni.

KAHNAWAKE MOHAWKS

Kahnawake, a Mohawk reserve just outside Montreal, has been the home of many Mohawks who worked in "high steel," constructing skyscrapers. It is also the birthplace of the Mohawk Warrior Society. The Warrior Society, started at Kahnawake in the early 1970s by Louis Hall, a Kahnawake Mohawk, was prominent in violence related to gambling and questions of tribal leadership at the Akwesasne (St. Regis) Reservation straddling the New York, Ontario, and Quebec borders and the occupation at Oka, Quebec.

During the early decades of the twentieth century, many of Kahnawake's Mohawks built bridges

The Sauk leader Keokuk, as painted by George Catlin. Keokuk was a rival of Black Hawk for leadership of the Sauk and Fox (now commonly known as the Sac and Fox).

KEOKUK (c. 1783–1848)

Keokuk (Watchful Fox) was a Sauk chief who was recognized by United States officials after he refused to support Black Hawk during the years before and after Black Hawk's War (1832). Born in the village of Saukenuk, Keokuk's mother was half French, so he could not be an hereditary chief. He obtained his position among the Sauk through merit, notably bravery against the Sioux, as well as political intrigue with invading non-Indians.

Division between Black Hawk and Keokuk had split the Sauk and Fox tribes before Black Hawk's War. Keokuk, attempting to maintain peace, moved his supporters from present-day Illinois into Iowa in 1820. In the early 1830s, Keokuk, with Fox treaty chiefs Powasheek and Wapello, signed a surrendering of the Rock River country for twenty thousand dollars in annuities and a tract of land in Iowa. In 1845, the land in Iowa was exchanged for a tract in Kansas.

After Black Hawk's War, President Andrew Jackson recognized Keokuk, instead of Black Hawk, as chief of the Sauk (Sac) and Fox. The news came to Black Hawk and Keokuk as they stood together with U.S. Army officers. Angry and frustrated, Black Hawk removed his loincloth and slapped Keokuk in the face.

Keokuk died in Kansas during 1848, probably of dysentery. He was buried in Keokuk, Iowa, under a statue erected in his honor. Keokuk's leadership role among the Sauk was then taken by Moses Keokuk, a Baptist preacher.

SEE ALSO:
Black Hawk; Sac and Fox.

KERESAN PUEBLOS

The Pueblo people of New Mexico are members of three distinct language families: Keresan, Zunian, and Tanoan. Seven pueblos speak the Keresan language: Acoma, Cochiti, Laguna, San Felipe, Santa Ana, Santa Domingo, and Zia. All are regarded as

A Keresan youngster, ascending the old trail to the "Sky City," as Acoma Pueblo, a mesa-top pueblo in New Mexico, is commonly known.

The Keresan pueblo of Acoma, in New Mexico, is probably the oldest continuously inhabited community in the United States, dating from the twelfth century C.E.

being part of the twelve southern pueblos. Population figures vary according to a number of sources.

Located west of Albuquerque, Acoma Pueblo has 378,113 acres (151,245 hectares) of land. The 1980 census reported a population of 3,592, and the 1989 Bureau of Indian Affairs (BIA) Labor Force Report listed it at 4,350. However, the 1990 census reported a population of only 2,435.

Acoma Pueblo dates from the twelfth century and is the oldest continuously inhabited settlement within the United States, excepting possibly some of the older villages of the Hopis. Called the Sky City, Acoma sits atop a 350-foot (106-meter) mesa. Only about fifty people now inhabit the ancient town year-round. It has no electricity or running water. Most of the Acoma people live in the nearby communities of Acomita, Anzac, and McCarty's. A visitor center with a museum, crafts shop, and restaurant is located at the foot of the mesa.

Cochiti Pueblo is located west of Santa Fe. The pueblo has 50,681 acres (20,272 hectares) of land. The 1980 census reported a population of 918, and the 1989 BIA Labor Force Report listed it at 921. The 1990 census reported the population at 1,199. Cochiti Pueblo leases land to the town of Cochiti Lake, which offers recreational services. Cameras are not allowed at the pueblo. Cochiti drums are well-known craft items made here, as well as pottery, jewelry, and storyteller figures. A portion of the original 1628 church can still be seen in the rebuilt structure.

Also located west of Albuquerque, Laguna Pueblo has 484,495 (193,798 hectares) acres of land. The 1980 census reported a population of 6,233, and the 1989 BIA Labor Force Report listed it at 7,542. However, the 1990 census reported a population of only 3,644. Laguna is the largest Keresan-speaking pueblo, composed of six villages—Old Laguna, Paguate, Mesita, Paraje, Encinal, and Seama. Each town has its own fair and feast day. A rich uranium mine was located here, and now the Laguna Reclamation Project is attempting to restore the mining site. Some of the villages allow photography.

The bell tower of the Catholic church at Acoma Pueblo. The Acomas and other Keresan Pueblo peoples of New Mexico have been influenced by the Catholic Church since Juan de Oñate's colonizing expedition in 1598.

Mary Trujillo, a potter of the Keresan pueblo of Cochiti.

a population of 609. Santa Ana Pueblo is often closed to the public except for several feast days during the year. Many of the residents live on farmland outside the pueblo.

The largest of the eastern Keresan-speaking pueblos, Santo Domingo Pueblo has 71,092 acres (28,437 hectares) of land. The 1980 census reported a population of 2,857, and the 1989 BIA Labor Force Report listed it at 3,446. The 1990 census reported a population of 2,851. Santo Domingo Pueblo is known for its turquoise and silver jewelry. Cameras are not allowed.

Zia Pueblo is located north of Albuquerque. The pueblo has 121,599 acres (48,640 hectares) of land. The 1980 census reported a population of 645, and the 1989 BIA Labor Force Report listed it at 694. The 1990 census reported a population of 613. Zia Pueblo is known for its orange-on-white pottery. The Zia sun symbol was adopted by the state of New Mexico and appears on the state flag. The pueblo overlooks the Jemez River. Cameras are not allowed.

— D. L. Birchfield

SEE ALSO:
Acoma Pueblo; Green Corn Ceremony; Tewa Pueblo; Tiwa Pueblo; Towa Pueblo; Zuni.

SUGGESTED READING:
Minge, Ward Alan. *Acoma: Pueblo in the Sky.* Albuquerque: University of New Mexico Press, 1991.

San Felipe Pueblo is located north of Albuquerque. The pueblo has 48,929 acres (19,572 hectares) of land. The 1980 census reported a population of 2,145, and the 1989 BIA Labor Force Report listed it at 2,398. The 1990 census reported a population of 2,248. San Felipe Pueblo known for its ceremonials; its Green Corn Dance involves hundreds of participants. No cameras are allowed.

Santa Ana Pueblo is also located north of Albuquerque. The pueblo has 61,931 acres (24,772 hectares) of land. The 1980 census reported a population of 517, and the 1989 BIA Labor Force Report listed it at 549. The 1990 census reported

KICKAPOO

The Kickapoos, whose name means "he stands about," are of the Algonquian language family and are closely related to the Sac and Fox peoples. At the time of first contact with Europeans, around

1667, the Kickapoo Nation lived between the Fox and Wisconsin Rivers in present-day southern Wisconsin. In 1765, the Kickapoos moved into what is today central Illinois and then eastward to the Wabash River, which forms part of the border between Illinois and Indiana.

The Kickapoos formed many alliances with Indian and non-Indian nations alike as they attempted to protect the integrity of their land and way of life. From 1811 to 1813, the Kickapoos joined the Shawnee leader Tecumseh in an alliance of Indian nations resisting non-Indian expansion westward beyond the Ohio River. They also supported the British against the United States in the War of 1812, and many also supported Black Hawk, the Sac and Fox leader, in his fight against the U.S. government in 1832. By 1837, about one hundred Kickapoo warriors were enlisted by the United States Army to fight the Seminoles in Florida.

In 1785, the Kickapoos entered into their first treaty with the United States—the Treaty of Greenville. Under the terms of other treaties—one in 1809 and one in 1819—the Kickapoos ceded their lands in Illinois and moved to reservations first in Missouri and then in Kansas, where some Kickapoos live today. Following the 1819 treaty, many Kickapoos were reluctant to again move to unfamiliar land, and so Kennekuk, their spiritual leader (also known as "The Kickapoo Prophet") and the head of a Kickapoo settlement along the Osage River in Illinois, succeeded in delaying the move for more than ten years by telling U.S. officials that he was still preparing to leave and would do so as soon as he was ready. Finally, under the terms of yet another treaty, this one in 1832, Ken-

U.S. troops under Andrew Jackson *(far right)* defeat British soldiers at the Battle of New Orleans in the War of 1812. Many Kickapoos joined the British as part of Tecumseh's pan-Indian alliance in an unsuccessful effort to halt westward U.S. expansion.

nekuk's band of three to four hundred people left their reservation in 1833 and took up residence on a second reservation along the Missouri River in eastern Kansas. (That land was opened to settlers through two separate treaties, one in 1854 and another in 1862. The 1862 treaty required that the Kickapoos accept the allotment of their tribal lands to individual owners, and their surplus lands were sold to a railroad company. Interestingly, the proceeds of the sale were to be used for the benefit of the Kickapoos in Kansas.)

A large segment of the Kickapoos who were forced to cede their lands in Illinois went to Texas and became allies of the Texas Cherokees. When the Texans defeated the Cherokees in 1839 and forced them into Indian Territory (present-day Oklahoma), the Kickapoos established a village within the Choctaw Nation. Another band of Kickapoos settled on the Canadian River (also in Indian Territory), and their men served as security for the Creek people against possible fights with the Comanches and other tribes of the Great Plains. In the early 1850s, a group of Kickapoos went to Mexico and are known as the Mexican Kickapoo.

During the U.S. Civil War (1861–1865), more Kickapoos went to Mexico, having lost nearly all of their property in an attack and defeat by Texans. After the war, the Mexican Kickapoos were accused of stealing cattle from across the international border in Texas. Also following the Civil War, the United States began trying to persuade the Kickapoos to return to Indian Territory. Finally, in 1873, the government conducted an illegal raid into Mexico and the Mexican Kickapoo were forced back into Indian Territory.

In 1883, the federal government assigned the Kickapoos to a reservation in Indian Territory, just west of the Sac and Fox Reservation. In 1891, the government made the Kickapoos give up their reservation and accept individual allotments. Rather than accept yet another "agreement" in which they would give up tribal lands to individual ownership, the Kickapoos resisted the allotment provisions and asked for a smaller reservation instead. When the United States went ahead with the allotments, two-thirds of the Kickapoo people initially refused to acknowledge their allotments or to accept any money under the allotment agreement. Ultimately, however, by 1895, the government enacted the policy of allotment on the Kickapoo Reservation, opening up land not only to Native owners but to non-Indian settlers and homesteaders as well.

By 1901, the Kickapoos were becoming established on their individual allotments and had resumed the order of tribal affairs. One of their chiefs during this period, a woman named Wah-Poho-ko-wah, was the last chief by right of inheritance under the old tribal law.

In the years since this tumultuous period, the Kickapoos have, like other Native peoples, become increasingly integrated into the fabric of the mainstream culture even as they have held on to their own identity. In their dealings with outsiders and the government, Kickapoos long held closely to their religious beliefs and resisted sending their children to government-managed boarding schools, preferring that the children stay on the reservation raising cattle and farming. And yet, like other Indian people, Kickapoo warriors fought in World War I and World War II; and between the wars, the Kickapoos were reorganized under the Oklahoma Indian Welfare Act of 1936 and obtained a charter as a federally recognized Indian Nation from the Department of the Interior. Although the largest number of Kickapoos live in Oklahoma, many of them still live in Kansas, Texas, and Mexico.

— S. S. Davis

SEE ALSO:
Black Hawk; General Allotment Act; Kansas; Kennekuk; Sac and Fox; Tecumseh; Texas.

KICKAPOO PROPHET

SEE Kennekuk.

KICKING BEAR (1853–1904)

Kicking Bear, an Oglala by birth, was a first cousin of Crazy Horse and fought with him in many of the battles of the Plains wars, including Custer's defeat at the Little Bighorn in 1876. Kicking Bear's father was named Black Fox, and his mother's name was Woodpecker, but his place of birth is not known. Kicking Bear married the niece of a Miniconjou Sioux chief and so became a minor chief himself. He paid bride price (a payment made to the family of a prospective bride) in horses stolen from the Crow, traditional enemies of his people.

During the winter of 1889, Kicking Bear was among a small group of Sioux who traveled to Nevada to meet with the Paiute holy man Wovoka and to witness the songs, rituals, and dances of the Ghost Dance. The Ghost Dance was a set of spiritual beliefs and visions that offered hope for a world restored to the way things were before the misfortunes that had befallen Indian peoples with the coming of the Europeans. Upon his return, Kicking Bear advocated the Ghost Dance at the Standing Rock Agency with the permission of his uncle, Sitting Bull.

James McLaughlin, Indian agent at Standing Rock and a long-time adversary of Sitting Bull, forced Kicking Bear to leave the reservation a few days after his arrival. Intensive Ghost Dancing continued anyway, leading to the incidents that sparked the December 29, 1890, massacre at Wounded Knee. After the massacre, a group that included Kicking Bear continued the Ghost Dance at White Clay, a settlement at Pine Ridge, into early January. General Nelson A. Miles ordered the White Clay encampment surrounded but was able to negotiate a peaceful surrender. Kicking Bear gave up his rifle to Miles's forces on January 15, 1891.

Kicking Bear's surrender, which involved about five thousand Sioux and others, is significant to history as the last formal subjugation of Native Americans by the U.S. Army. Following the massacre at Wounded Knee, Kicking Bear was among a number of Sioux who joined Buffalo Bill Cody's Wild West Show to tour the urban areas of the East Coast and Europe.

SEE ALSO:

Buffalo Bill's Wild West Show; Crazy Horse; Ghost Dance Religion; Little Bighorn, Battle of the; Sitting Bull; Wounded Knee (1890); Wovoka.

KICKING BIRD (c. 1835–1875)

During the last ten years of his life, Kicking Bird became the principal leader of the peace faction

Kiowa leader Kicking Bird, in a photo taken sometime between 1869 and 1874 at Fort Sill, in present-day Oklahoma.

within the Kiowa Nation. Very little is known about his early life, except that he distinguished himself as a warrior when a young man and soon came to be a person whom others looked to for leadership. His name, Tene-angpote, has been translated as "Eagle Striking with Talons" as well as "Kicking Bird," but the latter is the name by which he is best known. He was also called Watohkonk, "Black Eagle." He is known to have been the grandson of a Crow Indian who had been adopted by the Kiowas.

In 1866, upon the death of the principal chief of the Kiowas, Little Mountain (who was also known as Dohasan), Kicking Bird was one of the two leading candidates to succeed him. Little Mountain had come to the opinion that military resistance against Euro-Americans who were invading Kiowa land was futile and that the only hope for the survival of the Kiowas was to seek a lasting peace with the United States. Kicking Bird was deeply influenced by Little Mountain and represented a continuation of his ideas after Little Mountain died. The nation, however, was deeply divided, and the other candidate for principal chief, Satanta, represented a large faction that wanted to continue to defend their homeland against invasion. The nation, unable to choose between Kicking Bird and Satanta, settled instead on Lone Wolf to succeed Little Mountain as principal chief, but the division within the tribe remained unresolved.

Kicking Bird had been one of the Kiowas to sign the Little Arkansas Treaty in 1865, in which the United States and representatives of some of the Kiowas had agreed to establish a Kiowa reservation, and he was one of the Kiowas, along with Lone Wolf, who signed the Treaty of Medicine Lodge in 1867, which set the boundaries for the previously agreed-on reservation. However, a large faction of the Kiowas were not represented at these proceedings, and they ridiculed Kicking Bird for his continued arguments for peace. In 1870, at a Sun Dance on the north fork of Red River, some Kiowas publicly accused him of cowardice.

In response to these accusations, and in response to the wholesale slaughter of buffalos on the southern Great Plains by non-Native American commercial buffalo hunters, Kicking Bird led a force of about one hundred Kiowas into Texas, where they intentionally provoked an engagement with a force of fifty-four U.S. Army cavalry under the command of Captain Curwen McCullen. Kicking Bird won the battle for the Kiowas by devising a successful flanking maneuver, and he reasserted his reputation for personal bravery by charging directly into the soldiers, killing one of them with his lance.

Thereafter, no one questioned his bravery, but he was unable to unify the Kiowa Nation. In 1872, he and Lone Wolf led a Kiowa delegation to Washington, D.C., where they argued for the release of two Kiowa leaders from prison, Satanta and Big Tree. In 1874, Lone Wolf led the Kiowa war faction into league with the Comanche leader Quanah Parker for what became known as the Red River War. Kicking Bird was able to persuade more than half the Kiowas to stay out of the war. He led them to the Fort Sill Agency in Indian Territory (in today's southwestern Oklahoma), where they were protected by the U.S. Army during the war.

There, Kicking Bird persuaded Indian Agent Thomas C. Battey to establish the first school for the Kiowas. The United States regarded Kicking Bird as the principal chief of the Kiowas, and after the Red River War, the government required that he choose which Kiowa war leaders should be sent to prison at Fort Marion, Florida. Within a week after he had chosen Lone Wolf, a medicine man named Mamanti (Mamaday), and about seventy-five others, Kicking Bird suddenly died, on May 3, 1875. His friends said that he was poisoned by resentful followers of Lone Wolf and Mamanti. He was buried in the post cemetery at Fort Sill.

SEE ALSO:
Kiowa; Lone Wolf.

KIDWELL, CLARA SUE (1941–)

Choctaw-Chippewa scholar, teacher, and administrator Clara Sue Kidwell is director of the Native American Studies program at the University of Oklahoma. She was born in Tahlequah, Oklahoma, in 1941. She attended high school in Muscogee, Oklahoma. She received her B.A (in letters) and her M.A. and Ph.D. (in the history of science, in 1970) from the University of Oklahoma. Before returning to the University of Oklahoma in 1995 to become the first director of the newly authorized program in Native American studies, she taught at colleges and universities throughout the country.

She has taught at Haskell Indian Junior College in Lawrence, Kansas, where she was chair of the social science division, at the University of Minnesota, at Dartmouth College, and at the University of California at Berkeley. At Berkeley, she also served as chair of the department of ethnic studies and as associate dean of the graduate division. After leaving Berkeley, she worked for the Smithsonian Institution in Washington, D.C., before returning to her alma mater at the University of Oklahoma.

She is the author of many articles in scholarly journals and the recipient of fellowships from the Newberry Library in Chicago and from the Smithsonian Institution. Her books include *The Choctaws: A Critical Bibliography*, for which she was coauthor (published by the University of Indiana Press for the Newberry Library), and *Choctaws and Missionaries in Mississippi, 1818–1918* (published by the University of Oklahoma Press).

KING, BRUCE (1950–)

Bruce King was born on the Oneida (Wisconsin) reservation on November 2, 1950, as a member of the Turtle Clan. Noted for his work in the theater and arts, King graduated from the Institute of American Indian Arts in Santa Fe, New Mexico, and later attended the University of Chicago, Circle Campus, where he studied drama, writing, and theater. He also studied theater through the Native American Community Services Colleges.

King enlisted in the United States Army and served in Vietnam as a helicopter ambulance medic in the central highlands during the later critical stages of the war. Upon his return to the States, he became active in theater, working with the Native American Theatre Ensemble in New York City and later serving as the artistic director of the Echohawk Theatre in Chicago. From 1981 to 1992, King was the theater manager and artistic director for the Turtle Museum in New York, and from 1992 to 1995, he was a professor of theater arts and drama at the Institute of American Indian Arts in Santa Fe.

King's talents and experiences combine in his expressions of Native American traditions. He is married with three children and currently resides

Choctaw-Chippewa scholar Clara Sue Kidwell has returned to her alma mater, the University of Oklahoma, as director of Native American Studies.

in Santa Fe, working as a scriptwriter and fine artist in many media, from oils to lithographs. His fine art uses expressionism and abstraction to make artistic statements about Native traditional values and lifeways. King may be regarded as a transitional artist who bridges time by using modern materials and thinking within a framework of traditional values. His art evokes a sense of the past and yet takes a step into the future of Native America.

SEE ALSO:
Institute of American Indian Arts.

Metacom, a leader of the Wampanoags, was known to the Puritans of Massachusetts as King Philip.

KING PHILIP'S WAR

Metacom, known by the English settlers as King Philip or Philip of Pokanoket, was the son of Chief Massasoit, sachem of the Wampanoags. Massasoit saved the Puritan colonists from starvation upon their arrival in what is now Plymouth, Massachusetts. Massasoit died in 1661 at the age of eighty-one, and his son Wamsotta, or Alexander, succeeded him. Wamsotta died suddenly on the way home, after being summoned before the colonial governor to demonstrate his loyalty in 1662. Many of the Wampanoags, including Metacom, who was to succeed him, believed that Wamsotta had been poisoned by the English.

At age twenty-five, when the mantle of leadership among the Wampanoags fell to him, Metacom distrusted nearly all whites and was also known as a man who did not forgive insults easily. It was said that he chased a white man named John Gibbs from Mount Hope to Nantucket Island (off of Massachusetts) after Gibbs had insulted his father.

Metacom could see his nation being destroyed before his eyes. English cattle trampled Indian cornfields; farming forced game animals farther into the wilderness. Traders fleeced Indians, exchanging furs for liquor. The devastation of alcohol and disease and the loss of land destroyed families and tradition. The English repeatedly summoned Metacom to appear before them in Plymouth and Boston.

In an attempt to maintain his tribe's independence, he told the English, "Your governor is but a subject. I shall treat only with my brother, King Charles of England. When he comes, I am ready." Despite Metacom's efforts, the English greed for land caused new laws to be passed, one demanding that Metacom obtain the colony's approval before any land could be sold. As leader of his sovereign nation, however, Metacom demanded the right to sell land as he chose.

In this setting, suspicion began to arise, on both sides, that the other side was plotting for war. In 1674, a Harvard-educated Indian named John Sassamon was found murdered near Plymouth. Three Wampanoags were arrested, found guilty of murder, and hanged. Two protested their innocence, and one, hoping for mercy when his rope broke during the hanging, accused Metacom of the murder as part of a plot against the English. Despite his accusation, he was hanged anyway.

This English justice outraged Metacom, who believed the entire matter was a Wampanoag concern. He was again summoned before the colonial government. His participation in the killing could not be proved, and he was dismissed. His efforts to get the English to honor the original treaty between his father and the English settlers continued to fail; the English increased their efforts to force the Indians to accept their laws. Metacom found himself in the position of many Indian leaders before him, and many who were to come after him, of accepting his tribe's destruction by peace or by war.

After the hangings, Metacom began to ready his tribe and the allied tribe of the Nipmucks for war. Some of the English settlers in the outlying areas began to abandon their farms for the safety of Plymouth, while others stayed. In the village of Swansea, some Indians began to loot the abandoned homes. Some of the settlers who stayed fired upon them, and one Indian was killed. Thus, the first blood was drawn by the English. In revenge, the killer, his father, and five others were killed the next day, and the war began for real—but not as a result of plotting by either side.

Plymouth Colony called up troops, led by Captain Benjamin Church, as did Massachusetts Colony. Both tried to track down Metacom on his home ground, the Mount Hope peninsula that stretched into Narragansett Bay. They failed to find Metacom, and their forces split up. The men in the Massachusetts force went west into Narragansett territory in western Rhode Island. On July 15, 1675, they forced some minor leaders of the Narragansett tribe to sign a treaty, giving land to the English and agreeing to hand over any Wampanoags hiding with them. Believing that peace with the Narragansetts was secured, the troops then marched to rejoin with the Plymouth men. The Plymouth men, led by Church, had found Metacom's warriors in the Pocasset swamps across the bay from Mount Hope. The English discovered that they were greatly outnumbered and had failed at any chance of surprise. They only escaped total defeat by fleeing on a Rhode Island sailing sloop.

When the Massachusetts force arrived, they again tried to attack Metacom in the swamps and failed. They then tried to surround him, but he

An English artist's conception of a battle fought at Hadley, during King Philip's War.

escaped, and the war then spread throughout New England. In August, the Indians attacked Brookfield, Massachusetts, and held the barricaded villagers under siege for two days before retreating from English troops sent to save the village.

The English then managed to spread the war to other tribes by torching a friendly village of the Pennacooks to the north and attempting to disarm friendly Indians in the Connecticut Valley. About four hundred Christianized converted Indians, known as "Praying Indians," were exiled to barren Deer Island in Boston Harbor.

In early November, troops from the Plymouth, Massachusetts, and Connecticut colonies attacked the Narragansetts, claiming they were violating the July 15 treaty. On December 19, 1675, about one thousand colonists attacked a Narragansett fort near Kingston, Rhode Island. After a daylong fight in which the colonists lost seventy men and the Narragansetts lost approximately three hundred warriors and an equal number of women and children, the colonists retreated. The Great Swamp Fight effectively destroyed the Narragansetts, but the survivors joined Metacom and carried on the battle.

During the winter of 1675 to 1676, Metacom's confederation ripped a trail of fire and destruction through New England's ninety settlements, attacking frontiers everywhere in the region. The town of Lancaster, Massachusetts, was abandoned after an attack by the Nipmucks killed fifty; Medfield, about twenty miles (thirty-two kilometers) from Boston was burned. At one point, Metacom's warriors charged into Plymouth, the hub of Puritan territory. In all, about twelve towns were destroyed.

Not all of the tribes were committed to the fight on either side, but the Indian tribes who favored the colonists began to betray Metacom and his warriors. That winter, the governor of New York, Sir Edmund Andros, asked the Iroquois Confederacy Mohawks to attack Metacom's warriors who had moved northeast of Albany, New York. The attack by the Mohawks drove Metacom back into New England.

In July of 1676, Church's men captured Metacom's wife and nine-year-old son. Metacom was reported to have said, "My heart breaks, now I am ready to die. . . ." His wife and son were spared only to be sold into slavery abroad. By August, all of Metacom's warriors, their families, and friends had been killed or driven into hiding.

On August 11, 1676, an Indian betrayed the location of Metacom's small camp in Mount Hope, where he had been hiding in the swamp. Captain Church, his men, and their Indian allies surrounded the camp and attacked. Reports of Metacom's death vary somewhat. According to some accounts, Metacom was killed in an attempt to escape, and Church ordered Metacom's body to be butchered, his head and one hand given to the Indian allies who had shot him, and his body then quartered and hung in the trees, signifying that the war was over.

According to other accounts, when English soldiers found him, they dragged Metacom out of the mire, then had him drawn and quartered—that is, each limb was tied to a horse, after which all four horses were set off in different directions. His head was sent to Plymouth on a gibbet, where it was displayed much as criminals' severed heads were shown off on the railings of London Bridge. Metacom's hands were sent to Boston, where a local showman charged admission for a glimpse of one of them. And while this account has Metacom's head remaining on display in Plymouth for a quarter century thereafter, it also reports that the remainder of Metacom's body was hung from four separate trees.

In terms of deaths in proportion to total population, King Philip's War was among the deadliest in American history. About one thousand colonists died in the war; many more died of starvation and war-related diseases. An estimated three thousand

This undated engraving depicts the death of Metacom, also known as King Philip, on August 11, 1676.

Native Americans died, twelve hundred houses were burned, eight thousand cattle were killed. Every Native American nation bordering the Puritan settlements was reduced to ruin—those whose members, in happier days, had offered the earliest colonists their first Thanksgiving dinner. Many of the survivors—including Metacom's son and an estimated five hundred others—were auctioned off into slavery in Spain and the West Indies for thirty shillings each. This served two purposes for the colonists: it removed the Indians from the area, and it raised money to help pay their enormous war debts.

After the war, some of the remaining Wampanoags and the Nipmucks joined the Narragansett survivors. Others fled to the West, Canada, or joined the "Praying Indians." In 1950, the Narragansetts were given the right to vote in state elections. The Wampanoag Tribal Council is currently located in Gay Head, Massachusetts, and the Nipmuck Tribal Council is located in Grafton, Massachusetts. The Narragansett Indian Tribe is currently located in Charlestown, Rhode Island.

— J. D. Berry / B. E. Johansen

SEE ALSO:

Iroquois Confederacy; Massachusetts; Massasoit; Mohawk; Narragansett; Pequot War; Rhode Island.

SUGGESTED READINGS:

Church, Thomas. *Entertaining Passages Relating to King Philip's War*. Boston, 1716.

Eagle/Walking Turtle. *Indian America: A Traveler's Companion*. Third Edition. Santa Fe: John Muir Publications, 1993.

Drake, Samuel G. *The History of King Philip's War*. Boston, 1829.

Howe, George. "The Tragedy of King Philip," *American Heritage*, December 1958.

Mather, Increase. *A Brief History of the War with the Indians in New England*. Boston, 1676.

Slotkin, Richard, and James K. Folsom, eds. *So Dreadful a Judgement: Puritan Responses to King Philip's War 1676–1677*. Middletown, CT: Wesleyan University Press, 1978.

KING, THOMAS (1943–)

Thomas King, an Oklahoma Cherokee, was born in Tahlequah, Oklahoma, in 1943. His teaching career has included teaching Native American literature at the University of Lethbridge, in Alberta, Canada, and chairing the Native American studies department at the University of Minnesota. His writing career has included writing screenplays and acting in movie versions of his critically acclaimed novels, *Medicine River* and *Green Grass, Running Water*. He has also contributed to Canadian Native literature through his 1990 anthology, *All My Relations: An Anthology of Contemporary Canadian Native Fiction*.

Both of King's novels, *Medicine River* and *Green Grass, Running Water*, deal with Indian men trying to return home after long periods of separation from their Native communities; both contain strong, independent women characters. King has said that his subject is tragedy and his technique is comedy. In *Medicine River*, the humor in the book is displayed largely through dialogue and a meddlesome character by the name of Harlen Bigbear. Bigbear, although sometimes obnoxious, serves as a catalyst for the protagonist, Will, to return home. *Green Grass, Running Water* is a more experimental book, with many different storytelling streams running through it at the same time. The humor in the latter novel also comes from the dialogue, but the book as a whole is based more on unusual situations than *Medicine River*. Characters are placed in absurd predicaments, such as when five-hundred-year-old Indians, named after characters from American literature and popular culture, attempt setting the world straight. Among other things, they repair old, stereotyped television Westerns so that the Indians come out on top.

KIOWA

The Kiowas, a Great Plains people who number nine thousand strong throughout the United States, live primarily in communities in southwest Oklahoma. Once a hunting people, the Kiowas excelled in horsemanship. Prior to acquiring the horse in the 1500s, they were a small band who hunted in the great forests and mountains in what is today the northern United States. They used dogs hitched to a travois as their chief means of personal transportation and for moving tipi poles and other supplies. The Kiowas moved frequently, sometimes ranging across the Great Plains as far south as Mexico and as far north as Canada in pursuit of the herds of buffalo that served as their major source of food.

Around the same time that they began using horses to expand the scope of their hunting and other movements across the Plains, the Kiowas began experiencing other events that would have a dramatic effect on their lives. One of these was the coming of the sacred Sun Dance ritual of the southern Plains, into their lives. Even as the Kiowas were enjoying this new form of spiritual expression, however, they encountered a presence that would prove to be by far the most formidable obstacle they had ever encountered on the Plains: European contact. Unlike the natural elements and enemy tribes that had often plagued the Kiowas' sense of security, European and European-American explorers, settlers, and soldiers would become an unrelenting force of encroachment and trespass on lands that the Kiowas depended on for food and housing.

In the nineteenth century, the westward expansion of Euro-Americans brought increasing numbers of settlers into the area where buffalo once roamed by the millions. More and more, streams of wagon trains crisscrossed the Plains, devastating the Kiowas' hunting grounds even as the U.S. government began routinely opening Indian land for non-Native settlement. Confrontations between Indians and non-Indians were inevitable.

In the middle of this threat to the Kiowas came the wholesale slaughter of the mighty buffalo. A source of food and the materials that provided clothing and shelter to Kiowas and other Plains peoples, the buffalo became a form of recreation to white "hunters," many of them using trains to move through the vast herds and pick off the buffalo nearly to the point of extinction. And unlike Indian hunters, who put to use virtually the entire buffalo, Euro-Americans took only the hides and left the rest of the animal to rot on the ground. Soon, the Plains were littered with decaying carcasses as far as the eye could see. By the end of the 1800s, fewer than several thousand of the great beasts were left anywhere across the Great Plains.

With the virtual disappearance of the buffalo, the traditional Kiowa way of life was, for all practical purposes, over. Like many other Indian tribes, the Kiowas were at the mercy of their conquerors. So weakened were the Kiowas by the loss of their land and sources of food and comfort, even the slightest shifts in the natural elements themselves were enough to destroy them. Already weakened by disease and war, the Kiowas saw their numbers drop dramatically between 1833 and 1880.

Man for man, the Kiowas had proven themselves capable of handling most enemy encounters on the Plains. It had become increasingly difficult,

Kiowa leader Satanta, photographed at Fort Sill, in present-day southwestern Oklahoma. Satanta was a noted warrior and orator who resisted the invasion of non-Native buffalo hunters in the 1870s.

An undated photograph of a Kiowa woman and her child in a cradleboard.

Toro Mucho, a Kiowa leader, in an undated lithograph.

parents or guardians fill out the documents, listing the names of parents, grandparents, or great-grandparents. Once the forms are completed, the committee verifies family lineage, assigning, upon completion, tribal membership.

Like any sovereign nation, the Kiowa tribe maintains a unique relationship with the United States government. This relationship is achieved by means of treaties that continue to be held between the federal government and the Kiowas. Although these legal bonds have often turned out to be flimsy, the Kiowas have managed to keep peaceful relations with the U.S. government. Organized under a tribal constitution, tribal committee members, including officers, are elected and serve two-year terms.

Within their own tribal jurisdiction, the Kiowas maintain tribal courts and judicial processes. In order to conduct its internal affairs, the tribe may initiate laws within tribal lands. These tribal laws and the legal decisions that arise out of the application of the laws generally apply to tribal members only. When tribal laws, customs, and traditions seem to contradict one another, tribal elders are consulted. In the area of law enforcement, various state, local, and tribal law enforcement agencies work hard at the sometimes difficult task of coordinating efforts to provide protection to tribal members in Kiowa country.

Today, the Kiowa tribe runs several successful business enterprises, as well as a commission that regulates the taxation of tribal goods and services. One thriving business provides transportation services to an area covering several counties in Oklahoma. This business, like other tribal businesses, caters to tribal members in the community. The most successful economic ventures, however, are two that attract patrons from outside the tribe: bingo and tobacco. The tribal office in Carnegie, Oklahoma, employs seventy-five to one hundred employees; this number reflects an increase in the number of tribal employees that has kept pace with the growth of tribal business.

however, for Kiowa warriors to defend themselves against the well-trained and well-armed professional soldiers of the U.S. Army. Added to this disadvantage was the fact that there was now more at stake than man-to-man combat; fighting against soldiers now meant defending entire communities, including women, children, and older people, from attack. By the end of the turbulent nineteenth century, and with the end of their many battles of resistance against the army, the Kiowas' existence as a living, thriving culture upon the Great Plains was changed forever. They could no longer live as they once had.

Today, the Kiowas boast gains in tribal membership. To become an official tribal member, a person must first fill out the necessary documents and present them for approval to the appropriate tribal committee. In the case of newborn children,

Charles Eisenberger, a Kiowa dancer in traditional Kiowa powwow regalia.

The Kiowa tribe provides social, health, and education services to tribal members only, and the Kiowa Housing Authority administers a housing program for families that qualify. The housing program, which has been in operation since the mid-1970s, has constructed and maintained many homes in southwest Oklahoma.

While some Kiowas still own original land allotments, many others do not. Every year, sadly, Kiowa landholdings shrink. In a very short while, there will be very little land held by Kiowas, and the tribe has introduced recent legislation to buy lands to develop for future tribal businesses and expanding home building.

The Kiowas speak a language that has not been identified as belonging to any major Native language group. Unlike many Native dialects, Kiowa stands alone and is regarded by linguists as an "isolate." Some linguists find that Kiowa is closely related to the Tanoan language-speaking group of the U.S. Southwest. Although there are fewer fluent speakers of Kiowa today, recent studies show that more and more young people are seeking to learn Kiowa. In Oklahoma alone, education reforms in the public schools have helped bring many educators, linguists, and tribal speakers together to plan a language and teaching program that will help preserve Kiowa.

Currently, a great deal of work is being done to develop systems of writing Kiowa. Many scholars feel that the most respected and well-represented system for writing Kiowa is the one developed by Parker McKenzie. McKenzie is a Kiowa linguist who has cowritten a grammar text and devoted many years to the analysis and development of written Kiowa. Today, his writing system is taught at the University of Oklahoma. There, Kiowa and five other Native languages are offered for college credit; Kiowa also fulfills the language requirement for students in the University of Oklahoma's College of Arts and Sciences.

— G. Palmer, Jr.

SEE ALSO:
Buffalo; General Allotment Act; Lone Wolf; Oklahoma.

SUGGESTED READINGS:
Mayhall, Mildred P. *The Kiowas*. Norman: University of Oklahoma Press, 1971.

Wright, Muriel. *A Guide to the Indian Tribes of Oklahoma*. Norman: University of Oklahoma Press, 1951.

KIOWA-APACHE

The Kiowa-Apaches are now a part of the Kiowa Nation of Oklahoma, with tribal headquarters located in southwestern Oklahoma at the town of Carnegie. The Kiowa-Apaches are under the jurisdiction of the Kiowa-Comanche-Apache Agency of the Anadarko Area Office of the Bureau of Indian Affairs. In the 1950s, the Kiowa-Apaches held two seats on the twelve-member Kiowa-Comanche-Apache Business Committee. Elections for the Kiowa-Apache seats on the Business Committee were held every four years at Fort Cobb, Oklahoma. However, the Kiowas and the Comanches now have separate business committees, which function as the equivalent of tribal governments, and the Kiowa-Apaches have remained allied with the Kiowas.

The Kiowa-Apaches are an Athabascan-speaking people. The Athabascan language became widespread throughout the North American continent from northern Canada to northern Mexico. Its speakers include the Navajos and other Apache peoples of the Southwest. The Kiowa-Apaches are thought to have diverged from other Athabascans in the northern Rocky Mountains, while their Southern Athabascan relatives were in the process of migrating to the Southwest. The Kiowa-Apaches became allied with the Kiowas, who are thought to have lived near the headwaters of the Missouri River in the high Rockies. Kiowa-Apaches migrated to the southern Plains with the Kiowas, stopping en route for a time in the vicinity of the Black Hills. They have been closely associated with the Kiowas of the Great Plains since they first became known to Europeans.

The Lewis and Clark expedition met the Kiowa-Apaches in 1805 and recorded the first estimate of their population, giving them an approximate count of three hundred. The Kiowas and the Kiowa-Apaches eventually became close allies of the Comanches on the southern Plains. This alliance allowed them to dominate a huge area encompassing a region that is today the high plains of eastern New Mexico, the Texas and Oklahoma panhandles, and the high plains areas of western Oklahoma and western Texas, west of the crosstimbers. The Kiowa-Apaches, Kiowas, and Comanches played an important role in providing horses for the Northern Plains tribes. Thousands of horses, acquired in great numbers on raids that extended far into northern Mexico, were traded annually from the late eighteenth century to the mid-nineteenth century.

By a treaty in 1868, the Kiowa-Apaches joined with the Kiowas and Comanches on the same reservation in what is today the southwestern portion of the state of Oklahoma. A devastating measles epidemic killed hundreds of the three tribes in 1892. In 1901, the tribal estate was allotted to individual tribal members, and the remainder of their land was opened to settlement by non-Native American farmers. The Kiowa-Apache allotments are near the communities of Fort Cobb and Apache in Caddo County, Oklahoma. Official population reports for the Kiowa-Apaches put their numbers at 378 in 1871, 344 in 1875, 349 in 1889, 208 in 1896, and 194 in 1924. In 1951, Muriel Wright estimated their population in Oklahoma at approximately four hundred.

SEE ALSO:
Apache; Black Hills; Comanche; General Allotment Act; Horses; Kiowa; Lewis and Clark Expedition; Oklahoma.

SUGGESTED READING:
Wright, Muriel. *A Guide to the Indian Tribes of Oklahoma*. Norman: University of Oklahoma Press, 1951.

A young man of Kiowa-Apache and Comanche descent. Kiowa-Apaches have lived in close association with the Comanches since sharing the same reservation in 1868.

KIVA

In the Pueblo cultures of the Southwest, kivas are ceremonial rooms that are usually at least partially underground. They are thought to have developed from the ancient southwestern pit houses of the Mogollon, Hohokam, and Anasazi cultures. Construction techniques and the shapes of kivas varied between these ancient cultures, but kivas became important ceremonial centers for all of them. Kivas continue to be important ceremonial centers today in the cultures of the Hopis in Arizona and the Pueblo peoples of New Mexico, though there is variation in the use and number of kivas among the Hopis, the Zunis, and the Keresan- and Tanoan-speaking pueblos of New Mexico.

A kiva entrance at Pecos National Monument in New Mexico. Portions of the abandoned pueblo have been restored.

For the most part, kivas are places where only the men gather, though on occasion in some pueblos the kivas are used for community purposes that include women, such as rehearsing songs during a festival. Ordinarily, however, the kivas are the one place within the matrilineal Pueblo cultures where men can gather by themselves to discuss such things as the planting of crops, as well as to perform ceremonials.

Kivas are entered through a hole in the roof, by descending a ladder into the kiva. Each kiva has a small hole in the center of the floor, a sipapu, which symbolizes the emergence of the Puebloan peoples to the surface of the earth from the underworld. Benches are built along the wall, which is usually circular.

Kivas are off limits to tourists and to anyone not a member of the particular religious society that uses the kiva for its ceremonies. These societies are different from the clans of the pueblos. Clan membership cannot be changed, but among some Pueblo peoples one can change from one kiva to another. Practices and customs regarding kivas vary among the different Pueblo peoples. They do not like to talk about cultural matters associated with kivas.

During the late nineteenth century, United States authorities did not honor the sanctity of kivas. U.S. Army troops entered kivas and forcibly removed young men of school age to send them to government boarding schools. Attempts were made to suppress the religious practices of the Pueblos, but those practices endured and today they remain strong in the contemporary life of the communities.

SEE ALSO:

Anasazi; Boarding Schools; Hohokam; Hopi; Keresan Pueblos; Mogollon Culture; Pueblo; Zuni.

A portion of this mural has been restored in a kiva at Kua'a Pueblo at Coronado State Park, near Bernalillo, New Mexico.

KLAH, HOSTEEN (1867–1937)

Hosteen Klah, who became one of the most prominent Navajo medicine men, was also an accomplished weaver who exhibited his rugs at two world's fairs. He stirred controversy within the Navajo Nation when, principally through his weavings, he revealed certain details of healing ceremonials conducted by Navajo medicine men. These details had previously been kept within Navajo culture.

Klah came from a prominent family of Navajo leaders. His great-grandfather was Narbona, who had been an important military leader for the Navajos. His father was Hoskay Nolyae, and his mother was Ahson Tsosie of the Tsithahni clan. Hosteen Klah was born in October of 1867 at Bear Mountain near Fort Wingate in New Mexico Territory during a time when his parents and most of the Navajo Nation were prisoners of war in the Bosque Redondo concentration camp in eastern New Mexico.

As an infant, after the family returned to the Navajo Nation, he was known simply as Ahway Eskay ("baby boy"). *Klah*, which means "left-handed," became the next name he was given and is the name by which he became known. *Hosteen* is a term of respect for older men.

As a boy, when he was not tending his family's sheep, Klah learned weaving from his mother and sister. It was not common for Navajo men to be weavers (as opposed to some of the Pueblo people of New Mexico, where men are the weavers), but he soon demonstrated an aptitude for the art.

Also as a youngster, Klah was an apprentice to several kinsmen who were Navajo medicine men and with whom he studied Navajo healing ceremonials. His interest in learning the ceremonies stemmed from an injury he received as a boy. At that time, an uncle who was a medicine man performed the Wind Chant for him, followed by the Fire Ceremony. Klah had learned the Hail Chant by the time he was ten years old. He then learned the Wind Chant and the Bear Chant. Some of these ceremonies, which can last up to nine days, require that the participants memorize hundreds of chants and many sand paintings.

Klah studied for twenty-six years before he held his first Yeibichai Ceremony (also known as the Nightway Ceremony) in 1917 when he was forty-nine years old. He had begun learning the Yeibichai Ceremony in his youth from Hathile Nah-Cloie, who was acknowledged at that time to be its leading chanter. The Yeibichai Ceremony lasts for nine days, and there are seven different versions of it. Eventually, Klah learned five of the versions. After 1917, he was acknowledged as the leading Yeibichai chanter.

Klah worked with Mary Wheelwright and Franc Newcomb to record many of his songs and sand paintings. He also provided information to other scholars and anthropologists, including Gladys Reichard. Klah caused consternation among fellow medicine men in 1920 when he wove a rug based on one of the sand paintings of the Yeibichai ceremony. This had never been done before, and it created something of a furor. But Klah's prestige silenced the controversy, and sand painting themes became popular among Navajo weavers. Over the next two decades, Klah would weave a total of twenty-five such tapestries and would train two of his nieces in the art. His nieces, in turn, produced an additional twenty-five weavings.

Klah mastered the art of weaving and gained an international reputation as a Navajo weaver. In 1892, he had represented New Mexico by exhibiting his weaving at the Columbian Exposition World's Fair in Chicago. In 1934, he returned to Chicago to exhibit his weaving at the Century of Progress World's Fair Exposition. Upon his death in 1937, an art museum (now known as the Wheelwright Museum) was built in Santa Fe by his friend Mary Wheelwright to house many of his tapestries.

Hosteen Klah spent many years training Beaal Begay as his apprentice. But Begay died unexpectedly in 1931. With the deaths of Begay and Klah, many sacred Navajo prayers and rituals were lost. Their deaths were mourned throughout the Navajo Nation.

— D. L. Birchfield

SEE ALSO:

Bosque Redondo; Medicine Societies; Navajo; Pueblo; Shamanism.

KLAMATH

East of Oregon's Cascade Mountains lies a high plateau that is home to the Klamath and Modoc people. Klamaths traditionally relied on rivers and marshes for fish, mussels, waterfowl, and *wokas* (pond lily seeds). The total population of the aboriginal Klamaths, including the closely related Modocs, was approximately twelve hundred to two thousand prior to contact with Euro-Americans. A 1990 census numbers the Klamaths at over three thousand.

The Klamaths gathered during the winter in multifamily earth lodges with communal storage pits. Woven tule (rush) mats and baskets provided furniture, bedding, dishes, and storage space. Clothing consisted of woven fiber aprons and hats, as well as some fur garments. As the weather warmed, people traveled by boat to spring fishing stations. Summertime heralded their hunting and berry-picking season; wokas-gathering occurred in August, the beginning of the Klamath year.

Klamath society was organized around approximately seven units headed by chiefs, although shamans were considered more important to the people. A wide range of spirits were recognized within the natural setting. At important life changes, individuals often left the group to go to a significant spot and fast and pray. Marriages were formalized with gift exchanges between families, and upon death, a person was cremated in his/her canoe along with personal goods. The survivors retired to a sweat lodge for purification.

The Klamaths had no great use for horses in their traditional lifestyle; some horses and guns began to be used after the mid-nineteenth century primarily for raiding purposes. The Klamaths remained relatively isolated until the gold rush, when their land was overtaken by settlers. The Klamaths signed a treaty with the U.S. government in 1864 and were given a reservation of 1,104,847 acres (441,939 hectares) in present-day south-central Oregon. Under federal agency direc-

These Klamaths posed for this undated photo sometime in the early twentieth century.

tion, the Klamaths were to become yeoman farmers, but this was difficult given their land type and climate. Grazing and timber-related operations were more successful occupations.

The Klamaths had their lands allotted under the 1887 Dawes Allotment Act, but establishment of tribal rolls and land claims cases delayed final allotment until the turn of the century. The surplus lands, originally scheduled to be sold at auction, were retained in trust for the tribe, and a sustained-yield (continued periodic harvesting) logging operation provided annuities for tribal members. As with many other allotted tribes, Klamath lands quickly passed into non-Indian hands through sale and lease.

The Klamaths rejected the Indian Reorganization Act of 1934, which attempted to establish self-government for all Indian tribes. Deemed a tribe of comparative wealth and having assimilated into the local economy according to the U.S. Congress, the Klamath tribe was the second tribe scheduled for termination in 1954. Under vote, over 70 percent of tribal members elected to withdraw from the tribe, with the government purchasing their remaining land to create the Winema National Forest. Documents show that in 1956, many tribal members believed that they could remain in the tribe and also receive their proportionate share payment for their land. It was also clear that few tribal members understood all of the effects of termination: for instance, that hunting and fishing rights would be given up along with tribal recognition. The terminated tribal members each received $43,500 for their assets. The remaining 473 tribal members refusing termination became a part of the group trust operated by the United States National Bank, subject to federal supervision. Termination of the Klamath tribe was finalized in 1961.

A 1974 court case (*Kimbol v. Callahan*) reaffirmed the hunting, fishing, and gathering rights of the Klamaths on former reservation land. The Klamath Indian Restoration Act, passed on August 27, 1986, effectively restored federal recognition, rights, and privileges to the Klamath and Modoc tribes. However, this law did not return any lands to the tribe. A requirement of the act was the submission of a plan for economic self-sufficiency, under which the Klamaths are seeking a return of some 680,000 acres (272,000 hectares) of their former reservation as a land base for economic independence.

— M. A. Stout

SEE ALSO:
Dawes Commission; General Allotment Act; Indian New Deal (Indian Reorganization Act); Shamanism; Termination Policy.

LABOR, INDIAN CONCEPTS OF

A long-standing myth regarding American Indians held that the men were lazy and shiftless, while the women, who were virtually slaves, did all the work. Like many other widespread myths about American Indians, this one is utterly false. Native American societies from earliest times operated on the basis of a division of labor along sex lines. Thus there was men's work, and there was women's work. While specific details regarding specified chores vary from tribe to tribe, the general principle remains true.

The American Indian attitude toward work is expressed clearly in the Cherokee tale of Rabbit, the southeastern Trickster, a version of which evolved into the popular story "Bre'r Rabbit and the Tarbaby." In the old Cherokee tale, the animals had been suffering from a long-standing drought. At last, they decided to dig a well.

They started digging—all of them except Rabbit, who felt that he was above that sort of work. The other animals told him, "If you don't help with the work, you won't get to share in the water." The smug Rabbit replied that he didn't need their water. "I get all I need from the dew on the grass in the early morning," he said.

The well got so deep that the animals had to cut a path into the walls of the well in order to get down to the bottom and then back up again. At last, they found water. Then one morning, someone noticed footprints on the path. They looked like Rabbit's tracks, but the animals hated to accuse him without better proof. They decided to lay a trap for the culprit.

That night, they took some sticks and some sticky tree sap, and they tied the sticks together and made them look like a man. Then they covered

An early depiction of the Indian trade in beaver pelts. The introduction of a market economy for furs changed the lives of American Indians, eventually creating a dependency on European trade goods.

the sticks with the sticky sap. They left this "man" to stand guard on the path that led down to the well, and then they went on home to bed.

Sure enough, once everyone else had gone to bed, Rabbit came along to get his nightly drink of water. He looked around to make sure no one was watching. Then he started down the path toward the water at the bottom of the well. Pretty soon he saw what looked like someone standing in his way in the path.

He challenged the guard, and when he received no response, he pushed and shoved and got himself stuck fast. He stayed there all night, because he couldn't pull himself free of the sticky sap. In the morning, the other animals found him there, and then they knew for sure that he was the one who had been sneaking down into the well at night to steal water.

While they were trying to decide how to punish Rabbit for his transgression, he begged them not to throw him into a nearby briar patch. He could take almost anything else, he said, but he couldn't stand the thought of being tossed into the thorny briars. Naturally, the animals tossed him into the briars, and he laughed at them and ran away.

Rabbit got away without being punished very much, but the point of the tale is that he would not have gotten himself into trouble in the first place and would not have been ostracized by his friends had he done his fair share of the work. This is a tale designed to teach, and its lesson is that one must do one's share. It's an American Indian work-ethic tale.

To continue with the southeastern example, Cherokees have matrilineal clans, and in the early days, the women owned the property. That included the house and the garden plots. Most of the women's work then centered on the home. Perhaps the origin of the myth of the lazy males and

A carpentry class for Indian students at Hampton Institute, about 1890.

A sewing class for Indian students at Hampton Institute, about 1885.

the female drudges came from this simple fact, for the earliest European observers formed their opinions while visiting in Indian towns. Naturally, they saw women working and men taking it easy. Much of the men's work was away from the home. And much of it was arduous and extended, such as raids on enemies or long hunting trips. Therefore, when they returned home, they rested.

Women were homemakers, cooks, mothers, gardeners, hide processors, clothing manufacturers, gardeners, gatherers of wild plants, basket makers, and potters. They also ground corn into meal and gathered firewood. Men were primarily warriors, hunters, and fishermen, but clearing land and erecting buildings were also their responsibilities, and they were the manufacturers of tools.

Men were responsible for conducting ceremonies, and the annual ceremonial cycle was complex. Many men were also specialists. There were town officials, medicine people, weapons makers, traders, eagle killers, and wolf killers. (Among the Cherokees, wolves and eagles held a special significance and could not be killed by just anyone.)

Much of the work listed above was seasonal. The gathering and growing of plants is obviously so, but hunting is also seasonal. There was a winter buffalo hunt. There were spring fishing trips. And different plants were, of course, harvested at different times of the year.

It should be noted here that while the roles of men and women were clearly delineated and in many ways kept separate, an individual could choose to take the part of the opposite sex. In other words, if a woman chose to become a warrior, no one would stop her. And there were men who chose to live as women.

A Seminole woman in Florida. Despite the cultural influences of European trade goods, many traditional Native cooking methods continue to be practiced today.

The arrival of Europeans changed the Indians' work habits tremendously. European trade goods gradually replaced many Native-produced goods, and the European demand for pelts intensified the hunting and the processing of animal hides. Hunters stayed away from home longer and killed more animals than before. The entire process, involving both men and women, has been described as a "Native industry."

As the white population grew and moved closer to Native populations, and the mixed-blood population grew among the Indians, more changes took

Indian students plowing at Hampton Institute, 1879. Most Indian students could find only agricultural work upon their return home from school.

place. Among the Cherokees, for example, some individuals became plantation owners, merchants, politicians, teachers, preachers, and journalists.

In the Southwest, where Indians had been gathered around Spanish missions, many Indians had become cowboys. And later, when the Indian tribes of the northern Plains had been confined to reservations, the only employment available to many of the Indians was on nearby large cattle ranches. Significant numbers of Assiniboines, Blackfeet, and other northern Plains Indians became professional working cowboys.

During this same period, Indian children were being taken away from their homes and families and put into government boarding schools, where the emphasis was placed on basic English, Christianity, and menial labor. Girls were taught to be domestic workers, and boys were taught mechanical trades. Indians, having been deprived of their traditional ways of making a living, were being taught to take a place in the white man's world, but that place was to be at the bottom.

Even under these incredibly difficult conditions, some remarkable individuals prepared themselves for professional careers. General Ely S. Parker, a Seneca Indian, earned college degrees in both law and engineering, but because the state of New York refused to give an Indian a license to practice either profession, he wound up making his career in the military and in police work. Dr. Carlos Montezuma, an Apache, and Dr. Charles Eastman, a Dakota, both studied and practiced medicine.

In what is now eastern Oklahoma, the so-called Five Civilized Tribes, having operated their own school systems for some years, had produced any number of teachers, preachers, lawyers, merchants, journalists, physicians, and politicians, as well as blacksmiths, gunsmiths, farmers, and ranchers. Oklahoma statehood changed all that, however. The school systems operated by the five nations were closed down, and Indian students went to public schools along with white students. More often than not, they were counseled to drop out and get a job.

World War II brought major changes to American Indians throughout the United States, with many Native people, men and women alike, joining the military and many others taking war-related jobs and moving into cities. Following the war, the Indian population had shifted, so that more Indians were living in cities than in rural areas. This meant that the majority of Indian children were in public schools.

But whether they were in cities, on reservations, or in non-reservation rural areas, unemployment rates for Indians remained low. When Indian people did find employment, they generally found it in minimum wage jobs. In rural areas, Indians found seasonal work with harvesting crews. In some areas such as eastern Oklahoma, chicken-processing plants, large nurseries, and other employers of manual laborers found in the local Indian population a workforce similar to that of migrant workers but with the advantage that it remained local.

The early 1970s brought on a rash of government programs, and with the federal money came jobs with tribal governments, job training programs, and money for higher education. All of this changed the face of Indian employment once again. Large numbers of Indians, mostly male, became government bureaucrats, some qualified and some not. And many Indians, again mostly male, took advantage of job training programs to become qualified plumbers, electricians, and carpenters. Women took advantage of other programs, such as cosmetology and secretarial training.

The problem with the job training programs was that once an individual had finished a program and become qualified for employment, more often than not, there were no jobs available locally in that line. Most Indian people seem to prefer not to leave home to seek employment. The result was that people became qualified for jobs but remained unemployed. And because the training programs paid a monetary stipend, often the same individuals would go back to take another course.

Of all these programs, the higher education program seems to have been the most successful. In one year alone in the 1970s, Northeastern State University in Tahlequah, Oklahoma, graduated over two hundred Indian students, many of them being the first in their families to ever attend college, much less graduate. Many of those people have since found their ways into the public school system as counselors, teachers, and administrators.

Today there is good news and bad news. The bad news is that there are still areas with significant Indian populations where the unemployment rate is extremely high. The good news is that Indian people, both male and female, can be found working at virtually every kind of job and in every profession.

—R. J. Conley

SEE ALSO:

Berdache; Boarding Schools; Eastman, Charles; Five Civilized Tribes; Montezuma, Carlos; Parker, Ely; Tricksters.

LACROSSE

Lacrosse is a fast and furious sport that has been played in varying forms by many Native nations. Today's most popular and best-known version descends directly from the Iroquois of the Northeast. Using a long stick that was curved at the end and webbed with a net of leather thongs to catch and pass a ball, opposing teams guarded their goals at opposite ends of a playing field that sometimes stretched more than a mile (1.6 kilometers). Early French missionaries thought the sticks resembled a bishop's curved staff or "crosier" and so dubbed the game they observed "LaCrosse." The Mohawk word for the game is *tehonhtjikwa:ehks*, pronounced "day-hoont-jee-gwa-ecks."

Among the Iroquois, the game is often referred to as "the Creator's Game" because the contest and sportsmanship is important and pleasing to the Creator. However, the game was also used to settle disputes between villages or to ask the Creator for help, with hundreds of players competing on the field of play, resembling a battle. Injuries, often severe, were common, and the roughness of the game helped train young men to be warriors. Agility, speed, alertness, and quick reflexes were important both in war and on the playing field.

The popularity of lacrosse grew in the mid-nineteenth century, when teams of Iroquois players gave exhibition matches in the United States,

The Iroquois Nationals team at play in Hempstead, New York. The modern game of lacrosse has its origins in a similar Indian ballgame that was universally popular throughout the eastern half of the North American continent.

Canada, and Great Britain. England and Scotland organized lacrosse clubs that are still in existence. Unfortunately, Native teams were usually banned from playing in regular tournaments, even internationally, because they were usually unbeatable. In 1990, the Iroquois Nationals, with the flag of the Iroquois Confederacy flying proudly, played for the first time in open international competition in Perth, Australia, and won. The Iroquois Nationals have since remained unbeaten.

The sport's equipment has evolved from the original resilient ash or hickory sticks hand carved and steam bent, laced with rawhide and soft thongs, a hard wooden ball, and no player protections. Team members today are padded like hockey players and hurl hard solid rubber balls from aluminum sticks with composite hoops webbed with nylon laces. The sport is fast and rugged and includes women's

teams. The two forms today are field lacrosse, played on a large marked playing ground with goals like hockey, and box lacrosse, which is played in a smaller area, usually a hockey arena, during the summer. The game is played internationally and has long been popular as both an intercollegiate sport and an intramural sport at the college level. In recent years, a professional league has emerged, with games broadcast on ESPN.

SEE ALSO:
Games; Iroquois Confederacy.

LaFLESCHE, SUSAN

SEE Picotte-LaFlesche, Susan.

LANGUAGE FAMILIES

The first attempt to create a comprehensive scheme of American Indian language families was undertaken by Albert Gallatin in 1836. Gallatin, who was U.S. secretary of war, revised and expanded his scheme in 1848. In 1891, two separate studies were published. One was by John Wesley Powell, the director of the Bureau of American Ethnology. He restricted his scheme to North American Indian languages. The other study was by Daniel Brinton, whose scheme included the indigenous languages of both North and South America.

These attempts, and others, to classify individual American Indian languages into language families have created controversies among scholars. In the twentieth century, there are two schools of thought in this matter. The scholars representing one of the points of view are called traditionalists, and the others are called reductionists. The dispute is largely about the methods that linguists should use in arriving at their classification schemes.

Traditionalists argue that detailed comparative studies should be undertaken before a linguist declares that two or more American Indian languages are related to each other and should be grouped into the same language family. Classifying languages in the same family implies that those languages evolved from a common ancestor language at some time in the past. Traditionalists, therefore, create classification systems that have many different language families, because very few comparative studies of the kind that would satisfy the traditionalists have been carried out. For North American Indian languages, traditionalists' schemes ordinarily have dozens of different language families. Traditionalists do not argue that these many different language families are unrelated to one another. They argue only that no one has yet proven that any of these families should be combined and that the number of families should therefore be reduced.

A student at Rock Point Community School on the Navajo Nation in Arizona. Only in recent years have Native students been able to take instruction in their native languages.

Reductionists, however, argue that detailed linguistic comparisons are not necessary to show that American Indian languages are very closely related to one another. They argue that there is abundant evidence for reducing the number of families of American Indian languages to only a few.

Traditionalists also argue that only linguistic evidence should be allowed in arriving at language classification systems. The reductionists argue that there are many other kinds of evidence that can be helpful in arriving at language classification schemes because the ultimate aim is to determine which languages evolved from a common ancestor language. In this regard, they argue that such recent discoveries as testing the speakers of different languages for similarities in their DNA (mitochondrial deoxyribonucleic acid) can be important evidence in showing a common physical ancestry, which implies a common linguistic ancestry as well.

The dispute between traditionalists and reductionists developed in the 1920s between Franz Boas, a professor of anthropology at Columbia University, and some of Boas's former students, especially Edward Sapir. Boas represents the traditionalists, and Sapir represents the reductionists. Sapir's ideas can be found in his article on language families in the 1929 *Encyclopedia Britannica,* in which he argues that North American Indian languages can be classified into only six families. The article sparked intense debate between traditionalists and reductionists, which has continued throughout the twentieth century.

Most recently, in the late 1980s and 1990s, Joseph H. Greenberg, a professor at Stanford University, and one of his students, Merritt Ruhlen, have carried the reductionist point of view even further by proposing a classification system that places all North American Indian languages into one of only three language families. Their proposal is also supported by recent studies comparing physical similarities between different language populations. In addition to DNA, the factors that have been subjected to comparison have included blood serums, immunoglobulin G, and the Rh factor.

These studies imply that North America was populated at three different times in the distant past, by three different groups of people, with each group's arrival being separated from the others by thousands of years. According to their proposed language classification scheme, most of the Native languages of the Western Hemisphere evolved from the language spoken by the first group to arrive in the hemisphere, which they call Amerind. When that group arrived is a matter of speculation.

— D. L. Birchfield

SEE ALSO:
Bureau of American Ethnology.

LAS CASAS, BARTOLOMÉ DE (1474–1566)

The Spanish Catholic priest Bartolomé de Las Casas arrived in the West Indies during 1502, ten years after Columbus's first voyage. He became a constant critic of Spanish behavior toward Native peoples. On one occasion, Las Casas commented on the depopulation of the island of Hispaniola (present-day Haiti and the Dominican Republic): "[The conquistadores] have so cruelly and inhumanely butchered [the Indians], that of three million people which Hispañola itself did contain, there are remaining alive scarce three hundred people. . . . [T]he islands of Cuba, . . . St. John, . . . Jamaica, and the Lucuyan Islands . . . are now totally unpeopled and destroyed; the inhabitants thereof amounting to above 500,000 souls. . . . [F]or . . . Forty Years, wherein the Spanish exercised their abominable cruelties, and detestable tyrannies in those parts, . . . there have . . . perished above Twelve million of souls, women and children being numbered in this sad and fatal list; moreover I do verily believe that I shall speak within compass, should I say that Fifty millions people were consumed in this Massacre."

Although Las Casas was critical of Columbus and the resulting cruelties visited upon Native Americans by the Spanish conquest, he still gave Columbus credit for his God-given navigational skills in crossing the Atlantic so that Europeans could colonize other lands and peoples. However, Las Casas did not want gold; he wished, instead, to convert American Indians to Christianity.

This engraving, dramatizing Spanish mistreatment of Native peoples, appeared in a sixteenth-century book by Bartolomé de Las Casas, Spanish missionary and historian.

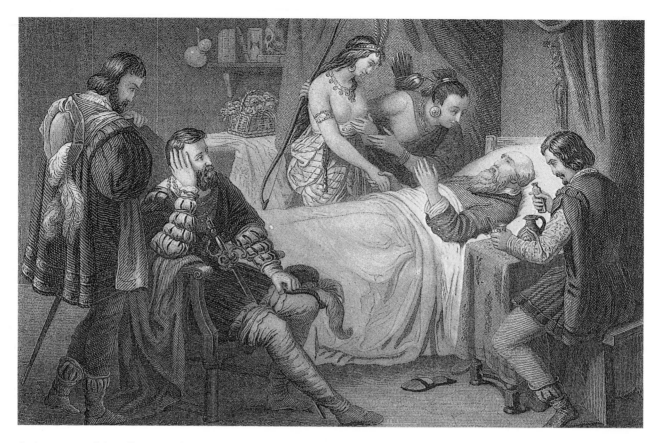

A depiction of the affection of Native peoples for Las Casas, as he lies on his sickbed.

His books were filled with graphic detail of the horrors of the Spanish conquest: "The Spanish found pleasure in inventing all kinds of odd cruelties, the more cruel the better, with which to spill human blood. They built a long gibbet, low enough for the toes to touch the ground and prevent strangling, and hanged thirteen [Native people] at a time in honour of Christ Our Savior and the twelve Apostles. When the Indians were thus alive and hanging, the Spaniards tested their strength and their blades against them, ripping chests open with one blow and exposing entrails, and there were those who did worse. Then straw was wrapped around their torn bodies and they were burned alive. One man caught two children about two years old, pierced their throats with a dagger, then hurled them down a precipice."

Las Casas wrote of Spaniards disemboweling children: "They cut them to pieces as if dealing with sheep in a slaughterhouse. They laid bets as to who, with one stroke of a sword, could split a man in two." In Mexico, he speculated that the Aztec Empire had been the most thickly populated area on earth before Cortés's conquest and diseases depopulated it.

While Las Casas's reports did little to stop the cruelty of the conquest, they did help influence papal declarations that Native Americans were to be regarded as human beings and not as beasts. Having found them human, Las Casas and other priests also found the Native peoples to be eligible for conversion to Christianity.

SEE ALSO:

Arawak; Aztec; Caribbean, Indigenous Cultures of; Columbian Exchange; Columbus, Christopher; Cortés, Hernán; Cuba; Hispaniola; Jamaica; Maya; Mexico, Indigenous Peoples of; Spain; Taino.

LATIN AMERICA

SEE Caribbean, Indigenous Cultures of; Central America, Indigenous Peoples of; Cuba; Hispaniola; Jamaica; Latinos; Mexico, Indigenous Peoples of; Puerto Rico.

LATINOS

Like the word *Hispanic*, *Latino* is often used today in the United States to refer to any person who comes from a Spanish-speaking ethnic background. Strictly speaking, however, unlike *Hispanic*, *Latino* also refers to people in North America whose Latin American background may be non-Spanish-speaking, such as Portuguese-speaking Brazilians. *Latino* is an umbrella term that includes many diverse peoples, from Chicanos (people of Mexican ancestry who live within the present-day borders of the United States) to Puerto Ricans, Argentines, Chileans, and many other different nationalities and ethnic groups. These peoples, like most other ethnic groups in North America, vary in their tastes in food, music, and art, in their use of Spanish, and in their political and religious views. Because of similarities in language and, for many, a shared experience of economic struggle and social hardship, however, most Latinos in the United States feel a bond.

While the largest number of Latinos who live in the United States are of Mexican ancestry and, along with Puerto Ricans, form the most visible Latino communities, substantial numbers of other ethnic groups and nationalities also have immigrated during the past few decades. Thousands of Cubans left their homeland after the revolution of 1959 and today live in many parts of the United States, especially in South Florida, where they are a highly visible and influential presence politically, socially, economically, and culturally. Almost every recent social and political upheaval in Latin America has sent refugees to the United States, including thousands of Salvadorans, Nicaraguans, Chileans, and others. Many Latinos, particularly Mexican-Americans and Central Americans, are of mixed Native American and European (usually, but not always, Spanish) heritage.

The Latino population of the United States is rising rapidly because of steady immigration and, compared to the rest of the population, relatively high birthrates. The United States Census has pro-

A student from Central America in a parochial school in Brooklyn, New York. Many Hispanic-American organizations are concerned with the well-being of Latino children.

Ray Barretto, a popular Puerto Rican percussionist. With their combination of Native, European, and African influences, Caribbean cultures have made significant musical, artistic, literary, and culinary contributions to mainstream North America.

jected that by the year 2050, the population of the United States may be about 390 million, of which 25 percent, or about 100 million people, may be Latino. Between 1980 and 1990, census reports indicated that the Latino population of California increased almost 70 percent. In Minnesota, Latino population increased 68 percent during the same ten years. In the United States as a whole, the number of Latinos counted by the census increased 53 percent, from 14.6 million in 1980 to 22.4 million in 1990.

During the late twentieth century, Latinos in the United States formed several hundred grassroots (self-help) organizations to deal with problems encountered in immigration, farmwork, and the transition from rural to urban ways of life. These groups are of several types, and most have specialized agendas, but almost all of them have been formed by Latinos with common economic and political problems.

Latino (principally Chicano) political activism has built a history of its own during the last half of the twentieth century. In the mid-1960s, Rudolfo "Corky" Gonzales formed the Crusade for Justice in Denver, typical of a number of local organizations that combined into a social movement in the 1960s and 1970s. In rural New Mexico, Reies Lopez Tijerina began organizing protests against the expropriation of Latinos' farm- and ranchland. The Brown Berets were formed in Los Angeles, a counterpart to the Black Panthers, an African-American activist group. Chicano studies departments began to emerge at colleges and universities, especially in the Southwest. In the late 1960s, a national political party, La Raza Unida, began to organize in some of the same areas. While the Latino population was overwhelmingly rural until midcentury, by 1990, roughly 85 percent were living in urban areas that had become major centers of Latino political activism.

A Mexican-American man in Chicago, surrounded by a mural inspired by Mexico's rich Native traditions.

This Mexican-American boy lives in the upper Midwest, but his western-style clothing reflects a cultural heritage that is both Native and Anglo-American.

Political activism in Latino communities has roots in a desire to gain education and employment, to escape poverty, and to maintain social and cultural traditions. Activists are trying to address problems such as the fact that 40 percent of Latino children (according to the Children's Defense Fund) were living in poverty by 1993. Indeed, social problems seemed to accumulate faster than activists could deal with them. In 1990, according to the CDF, a million more Latino children lived in poor families than in 1980.

Permanent grassroots organizations have formed in both rural and urban areas. Rural organizations usually have been formed to address the low pay and hazardous conditions of migrant farm labor. The United Farm Workers (UFW), organized in the 1960s by Cesar Chavez, used a combination of grassroots organizing tactics combined with traditional union-organizing strategies, such as strikes and boycotts. By the 1990s, farmworker unions had formed in various states and regions of the United States, including Florida, Texas, Washington, and Ohio.

By the early 1990s, membership in the United Farm Workers had declined from a peak of sixty thousand in the 1970s to about five thousand. Farmworkers were granted the right to collective bargaining and redress for unfair practices on the job by federal legislation in 1975. By 1993, however, the union that had tried to realize these rights had been slowly broken by the growers, while state agencies with the same job had been closed or reduced during California's state budget crisis.

Although its use is illegal in California, farmworkers report that more growers were forcing them to use the infamous *cortito*, the short-handled hoe that has condemned many people to excruciating back pain in later life. The cortito became a trademark of oppression during the UFW-organizing years. Workers reported in the early 1990s that some growers were forcing those who would not weed with the short hoe to use their hands instead.

In many urban areas, especially in the western United States, grassroots groups formed to bring together many Latinos who had migrated to urban areas as farmwork became mechanized. Some grassroots organizations formed during the Chicano movement of the late 1960s and 1970s had achieved substantial size and permanence by the 1990s. In the city of Seattle, Chicanos and supporters from other ethnic groups occupied an abandoned school in the fall of 1972 and gradually began to renovate it with their own labor. Twenty years later, El Centro de la Raza had become a large social-service organization with an annual budget of several million dollars, worldwide activities, and several dozen salaried employees.

Some political activism is undertaken to support Mexican workers being exploited in the United States. In 1993, Mexicans were being recruited to North Carolina to pick and pack crabmeat with promises of high pay ($250 a week take-home) and their own clean houses with Spanish-language cable TV, phones, washers, and dryers. They got substandard housing, none of the promised amenities, and paychecks riddled with so many penalties and deductions that one woman ended up with $15 after working a forty-nine-hour week. The workers were housed in two run-down houses near the crab plant, assigned two to a bed. The rents that they were charged added up to $2,400 a month per house. Everything that the labor recruiters had done was legal under U.S. law.

Other grassroots organizations have formed to address problems of immigration that arose with the rapid influx of Latin American nationals into the United States, either legally or illegally. While some of these groups have formed permanent structures with offices, boards of directors, and substantial budgets, others have been formed to face a single issue in a single place.

Late in 1992, for example, Latino citizens in Omaha, Nebraska, formed a specific effort after two Mexican teenagers, Ambrosio Lopez and Agustín Antuñez, were arrested November 6, 1992, at South High School (in the Latino community) and deported to Mexico by the Immigration and Naturalization Service (INS). These arrests differed from most INS raids in that they happened in a public school and in that the INS deported children whose parents were United States citizens.

This effort brought together clergy in churches with Latino congregations, school officials, the editors of Omaha's bilingual newspaper *Nuestro Mundo*, Latino business owners, immigration-rights lawyers, and eventually Nebraska's governor, Ben Nelson. The organizers even brought the time of the year—the weeks before Christmas—into the struggle. After considerable haggling on a national

Looking very amused and obviously enjoying a day of entertainment, these young Mexican-American women share a laugh at an outdoor festival in Chicago.

level, Governor Nelson announced the return of the two boys at a press conference on Christmas Eve.

Activity in Spanish and bilingual (English-Spanish) publications and broadcasting exploded late in the twentieth century in the United States and Canada. Many Spanish or bilingual newspapers were started in urban areas, often beginning as small businesses. Other Latinos were finding work in the mainstream journalism, although by the mid-1990s, the number of Latinos employed in mainstream newspapers, television, and radio still did not match their proportion of the general population.

Latino journalism has experienced an explosion of activity as a career option late in the twentieth century. A rising number of weekly and monthly Latino community newspapers and a number of new magazines were tied together by the Hispanic Link News Service, which provides news, columns, cartoons, and commentary from Washington, D.C. Some cities even have competing papers. Some are principally advertising vehicles, while others have political and social motivations. By the middle 1990s, most urban areas in the United States hosted at least one newspaper that published in Spanish, or in English and Spanish. Many were begun on shoestring budgets. Most of these papers publish a general menu of community news, from articles describing community members serving in the armed forces to marriages, deaths, and school honor rolls. Many of these papers also maintain a strong activist stance, particularly through their editorial columns, in which the paper may take on controversial subjects, such as the shooting death of a Mexican immigrant or a state's English-only laws.

— B. E. Johansen

SEE ALSO:
Aztec; Caribbean, Indigenous Cultures of; Central America, Indigenous Peoples of; Cuba; Maya; Mexico, Indigenous Peoples of; Puerto Rico.

SUGGESTED READINGS:
Gonzales, Sylvia Alicia. *Hispanic-American Volunteer Organizations*. Westport, CT: Greenwood Press, 1984.
Marzolf, Marion, and Melba Tolliver. *Kerner Plus 10: Minorities and the Media: A Conference Report*. Ann Arbor: University of Michigan School of Journalism, 1977.
Smith, Darren L., ed. *Hispanic Americans Information Directory*. Detroit: Gale Research, 1991.
United States Census. *Population Reports, 1970, 1980, 1990*. Washington, DC: Government Printing Office.
Wilson, Clint C., II, and Felix Gutierrez. *Minorities and Media: Diversity and the End of Mass Communication*. Beverly Hills: Sage, 1985.

LEAGUE OF THE IROQUOIS

SEE Iroquois Confederacy.

LEDGER ART

In the nineteenth century, long, narrow, leather-bound books with lined paper were used by storekeepers, merchants, traders, and military officers to keep accounts of business. These ledger books often found their way into Native hands and were used to create highly stylized pictographic drawings.

The most common images were called "exploits"—depictions of warfare, the hunt, or romantic scenes such as a courtship. The images, though sometimes simple, reveal much about the complexities of Northern Plains Indian culture.

Traditionally, women painted or drew geometric designs, and men painted pictographic or realistic designs, such as were found on buffalo robes or tipi liners. But all ledger art was created by men and usually dates to the late reservation period from about 1875 to 1900.

Much of the ledger art created on the Northern Plains was done for government Indian agents as gifts and to illustrate what was rapidly becoming a fading way of life. Native people were given pens and colored pencils, and some ledger works were actually commissioned by officers who took them back East as souvenirs. However, many Native people were incarcerated in prisons like Fort Marion, Florida, where the ledger art expressed feelings of homesickness and loneliness. Some prison collections are very famous, including *Fort Marion Book*, *The Howling Wolf Ledger*, and *The Short Bull Book*.

Two examples of ledger art , both from around 1880. One *(top)* is by Julian Scott (Kiowa); the other *(bottom)* is by Howling Wolf (Southern Cheyenne). They are done in colored pencil, ink, and crayon.

The nations most commonly associated with ledger art are the Lakota (Sioux), Cheyenne, Crow, Arapaho, Kiowa, and Gros Ventre. Many notable Native Americans, including Sitting Bull (Lakota) and Medicine Crow (Crow), were skilled artists with a fine eye for detail, perspective, color, and balance.

This particular style of art was also done in a cruder form by boys removed from their families and sent to government boarding schools like Carlisle or Haskell. Ledger art has evolved into modern Native arts that express traditional values in a changing world.

SEE ALSO:

Boarding Schools; Carlisle Indian School; Haskell Indian Nations University.

LEFT HAND, THE ELDER
(1820s–1864)

Left Hand's name in the Southern Arapaho language has been variously spelled as Nawat or Niwot, and it translates simply as "left-handed." Left Hand was an important chief in the Southern Arapaho Nation during the mid-nineteenth century, though he was not the principal chief. He is known to have been a strong advocate for peace on the southern Great Plains during the time that gold miners were intruding on lands of the Southern Arapahos and Southern Cheyennes, especially in the area of the front range of the Rocky Mountains in present-day Colorado. At that time, Denver was a booming mining town, and the unruly miners caused the Indians in the region many problems.

The Southern Arapahos and the Southern Cheyennes were closely allied and frequently shared the same camps. In the middle of the nineteenth century, Black Kettle was the leading chief among the Southern Cheyennes, and in 1855, Little Raven succeeded his father as the principal leader of the Southern Arapahos. Left Hand, who had learned English from his sister's husband, was an important translator for both the Southern Cheyennes and the Southern Arapahos in their dealings with the United States and its many citizens who were pouring into the region.

Left Hand disappears from the historical record after 1864, and he was apparently killed as one of the Southern Arapahos who were camped with Black Kettle's band of Southern Cheyennes at Sand Creek in 1864 when a contingent of Colorado Volunteers under the command of Colonel John M. Chivington attacked the camp and massacred most of its inhabitants.

Left Hand has frequently been confused by historians of the Plains Indian wars with a much younger Southern Arapaho leader of the same name who succeeded Little Raven as principal chief of the Southern Arapahos in 1889. The younger Left Hand served in that capacity until his death in 1911. It is not known if the two men called Left Hand were related.

SEE ALSO:

Black Kettle; Left Hand, the Younger; Sand Creek Massacre; Wars, Indian.

LEFT HAND, THE YOUNGER
(c. 1840–1911)

Very little is known about the early life of Left Hand, except that he was born somewhere on the southern Great Plains about 1840 in one of the camps of the Southern Arapahos and that he never learned the English language. Like an earlier important Southern Arapaho chief, his name has been variously spelled as Nawat or Niwot and means "left-handed."

He might have been one of the Southern Arapaho leaders who accompanied their principal chief, Little Raven, on a trip to the eastern seaboard in 1871. On that trip, Little Raven made an impassioned speech for fair treatment of the Plains Indians by the United States to an audience at Cooper Union in New York City.

When Little Raven died in 1889 at the age of seventy-two, Left Hand succeeded him as principal chief of the Southern Arapahos. By that time, the Southern Arapahos had been forced to give up all of their claims to much of the southern Great Plains in the region of eastern Colorado, western Kansas, and western Nebraska and to accept the confines of a reservation in what is now central and western Oklahoma. But even this small remaining area was under attack by the Congress of the United States, through the vehicle of the Dawes Commission and government pressure that would force the Indian nations in Oklahoma to allot their tribal lands to individual tribal members and open the surplus to white settlement.

Left Hand made numerous trips to Washington, D.C., on behalf of his people, and he gained a reputation for a willingness to compromise and a keen reasoning ability that helped his people make a smoother transition to reservation life than many other tribes. But on one trip to Washington, D.C., in 1890, he created controversy within his nation and within the Southern Cheyennes, with whom the Southern Arapahos shared their reservation, when he signed an agreement that allowed for the allotment of the Southern Arapaho lands in Indian Territory (present-day Oklahoma).

After small portions of the Indian lands in Indian Territory had been allotted to tribal members, land runs were held for white settlers to claim the large surplus. The white population soon overwhelmed the Indians, and Oklahoma was admitted to statehood in 1907. Left Hand and the other Southern Arapahos were told by the United States that their nation no longer existed and that they had become citizens of the state of Oklahoma. Not until the 1970s would the United States change its attitude toward the Indians in Oklahoma and again deal with the Southern Arapahos in a government-to-government relationship. By then, Left Hand had been dead for more than half a century. He died near Geary, Oklahoma, on June 20, 1911.

SEE ALSO:

Dawes Commission; General Allotment Act; Left Hand, the Elder; Oklahoma.

LENAPE

The Lenape or Delaware Indians at one time occupied an area of approximately twenty-five thousand square miles (sixty-five thousand square kilometers) along the eastern coast of the United States. Their homeland consisted of the present state of

Nora Thompson Dean, a Lenape woman living in Oklahoma, in her kitchen preparing white flour corn for making corn-in-the-milk bread.

along the Delaware River, which had been named after Lord de la Warr. The term *Lenni Lenape*, often seen in books, is rarely used by Lenape speakers, as it is considered redundant.

Throughout their homeland, the Lenapes had a number of independent villages and at least three major dialects of their language. Of these earlier dialects, only Unami, spoken in Oklahoma, and Munsi, spoken in Canada, remain.

In each village were three major divisions by clan. All Lenapes inherited their clan affiliation through their mother. The three clans were the Tùkwsit (Wolf clan), Pële (Turkey clan), and Pùkuàngo (Turtle clan). Each clan may have had further subdivisions, but specific information on such divisions at that early date is lacking.

The daily activities of the Lenape people were divided fairly between the men and the women. The men's responsibilities consisted of

A 1918 portrait of James F. Buffalo, a Lenape corporal in the U.S. Army during World War I. Like many other Native Americans, Corporal Buffalo fought valiantly for the United States, even though Congress would not pass a law making all Indians U.S. citizens until 1924.

hunting and fishing (not to be confused with hunting and fishing as the sports they are today), thus providing the sole source of meat. The men also had the responsibility of preparing the houses, making dugout canoes, fashioning stone and wooden implements, clearing new fields of trees, and doing other heavy work. The women's work consisted of cooking, making clothing of deer hide and other materials, tanning the hides, gardening, pottery making, basketry, and performing other chores pertaining to the necessities of a household. In Lenape society, the house was considered the property of the woman.

New Jersey, the eastern part of Pennsylvania, the northern part of Delaware, and southeastern New York. Some believe that the Lenapes may have resided in their homeland for thousands of years before the arrival of the Europeans.

Lenape, which means "common people," is the name they call themselves. They also became known as the Delaware because many of them lived

Initial contacts with the Europeans (the Swedes, Dutch, and English) were for the most

In this 1975 photo, a Lenape man poses at the archery stand he runs at Native dances and other events, charging a small fee for Indian and non-Indian customers to test their skill with a bow and arrow.

A young Lenape boy named Lewis Bullett poses for an old-fashioned sepia portrait in traditional Delaware clothing. This picture was taken in 1977.

Lenapes thought they were just granting permission for temporary use of the land. The Europeans began to take possession of the land, and as early as the middle 1600s, some Lenapes were forced to leave their old homeland.

Often the land was acquired by dishonest means, such as the infamous "Walking Purchase," which took place in 1737. William Penn had always dealt fairly with the Lenapes, but after he returned to England, his sons and other agents began to sell land to pay their creditors. These were lands still owned by the Lenapes.

In order to convince the Lenapes to part with the land, the Penns falsely represented an old incomplete and unsigned draft of a deed as a legal contract. They told the Lenapes that their ancestors some fifty years before had signed this document, which stated that the land to be deeded to the Penns was as much as could be covered in a day-and-a-half's walk.

Believing that their forefathers had made such an agreement, the Lenape leaders agreed to let the Penns have the area walked off. They thought the whites would take a leisurely walk down an Indian path along the Delaware River. Instead, the Penns hired three of the fastest runners, and had a straight path cleared. Only one of the "walkers" was able to complete the "walk," but he went fifty-five miles (eighty-nine kilometers).

part friendly, and both sides entered freely into the spirit of trading. But the Europeans also wanted to buy Lenape lands. The Lenapes did not know that the European tradition was that they could purchase land for their own unshared ownership. The Lenapes felt that the land belonged to the Creator, who let the people use it; it could no more be sold than one could sell the air. The

And so by means of a false deed and the use of runners, the Penns acquired 1,200 square miles (3,120 square kilometers) of Lenape land in Pennsylvania, an area about the size of Rhode Island! The Lenapes complained about the way the "walk" had been done, but they felt honor bound to fulfill what they thought their ancestors had agreed to.

Over the next 250 years, the Lenapes settled in many new places, each time believing this was to be their home from that time forward, but they were soon forced to move again westward. Their first move was into central Pennsylvania along the Susquehanna River, then western Pennsylvania, then Ohio, then Indiana, then Missouri, and then Kansas. Finally, in 1867, they moved to Indian Territory, now called Oklahoma. This group presently numbers over 10,200 and has its headquarters at Bartlesville, Oklahoma. Members from the group reside all over the United States.

A splinter group left the main group of Delawares in 1795 and traveled down through Louisiana into Texas, where they lived for some time, but they were forced to move up into western Oklahoma, where they are located at the present time. Three other groups of Lenapes moved into Canada and settled in southern Ontario, where they are to be found to this day at Moraviantown and Muncey and on the Six Nations Reserve.

Some people of Lenape descent continue to reside in the East in the original homeland, and although they do not have federal recognition, they have been able to use historical documentation to authenticate their people as being of Lenape descent. Most Lenapes from the recognized groups have no quarrel with people who have been told that in their family's lineage there was a Lenape ancestor. Unfortunately, the great interest in Lenape life has also brought out a number of non-Indians claiming to be not only Indian, but also chiefs, medicine people, and so forth. These people often have some made-up "ceremonies" with which to fool the public.

The main religious activity of the Lenape people was centered around Xingwikaon, or Big House Church. Meetings were held in this large building every fall to give thanks to the Creator for the crops, good hunting and fishing, and so forth. This was also a time to ask the Creator for blessings on them for the year to come.

In the Lenape belief, there was one Supreme Being under whom served a number of lesser spirits called manìtuwàk. The Supreme Being was believed to reside in the twelfth layer of heaven, while some of the lesser manìtuwàk resided in the other eleven layers. For example, the thunderbirds who bring the rain are said to live in the first layer of heaven.

The Lenapes also had a number of religious ceremonies of lesser importance. Some of these ceremonies, such as the Doll Dance, the Otter Hide Dance, the Bear Dance, the Green Corn Dance, and the Mësingw (or "guardian of the game animal") Dance have been lost because of pressure from missionaries and Euro-American culture in general.

Some Europeans arriving in the Americas felt an obligation to "civilize" the Native people. One way of accomplishing this was to eradicate the Native languages and culture. In later times, in government-run Indian schools, Indian students, including many Lenapes, were punished for even trying to speak their tribal language or wearing any item of clothing or jewelry that was of Native origin. The teachers made efforts to totally erase any knowledge of Native culture and to make Native people forget they were Indian. Sadly, these efforts sometimes resulted in some students becoming embarrassed about their ancestry.

As many present-day Lenapes will attest, such attempts to turn Indians into well-tanned whites have been only partly successful. In spite of the loss of the older ceremonies, since the late 1960s the Lenapes have witnessed a surge of interest in their traditional heritage. People who had been swayed into forsaking their Indian heritage have now returned to take part in traditional ways and are relearning the language and ways of their ancestors. There are still some ceremonies and a number of Lenape dances with names like Raccoon Dance, Duck Dance, Bean Dance, Go-Get-'Em Dance, War Dance, and others. These continue today and will hopefully be around for many more generations.

— J. Rementer

SEE ALSO:

Big House Church; Boarding Schools; Ceremonies, Exploitation of; Penn, William; Walking Purchase.

LEWIS AND CLARK EXPEDITION

In January of 1803, President Thomas Jefferson proposed an exploratory journey into the far West, "even to the Western Ocean." He suggested that an officer and ten or twelve men could make the trip for about $2,500. The purpose of the exploration, Jefferson said, was to extend the commerce of the United States, since Indians in the far West were selling their furs to either the British Hudson's Bay Company or the Northwest Company of Canada.

Congress approved the proposal in February, in spite of the fact that France, Britain, and Spain held claims to various parts of the territory in question. Then, in April, the United States and France concluded the deal known as the Louisiana Purchase. While it was not an actual land purchase, but rather a purchase of France's recognized exclusive right to negotiate with the Native population for their lands, the U.S. began to behave as if it had actually bought the land itself.

Jefferson moved ahead with his plan for exploration with the organization of what he called the "Corps of Discovery," but that has become known in history as the "Lewis and Clark Expedition." The president appointed his private secretary, Meriwether Lewis, as the leader of the corps. Lewis chose William Clark, younger brother of the famous George Rogers Clark, as second in command. Lewis assembled all the equipment for the journey, while Clark recruited and trained the men.

On May 14, 1804, the expedition left Camp Dubois, near St. Louis, moving northwest on the Missouri River with a keelboat and two pirogues. (A pirogue is a canoe made out of a hollowed-out tree trunk.) The company was made up of twenty-six soldiers and two civilians.

Lewis and Clark made copious notes along the way regarding the animal and plant life they encountered and, of course, the Indians they met. The first Indians they met and talked with were Otos at what is now Council Bluffs, Iowa. They distributed gifts and peace medals with the likeness of Jefferson on them. Then, Lewis made a threatening speech, issuing orders from "the great father," who, he said, "could consume you as the fire consumes the grass of the plains." Following his speech, Lewis fired off his now famous "toy," an experi-

mental air rifle that he claimed was magic, as it required no gunpowder to be fired.

They traveled farther up the river to a place near present-day Sioux City, Iowa, where Sergeant Charles Floyd died of an intestinal disorder. Remarkably, Floyd was the expedition's only casualty, and today a monument marks the site of his death and burial.

Farther upriver and following two cases of disciplinary actions against soldiers (both of whom were severely beaten and then discharged from the corps), the expedition encountered a band of Teton Sioux. After a brief talk, the two parties faced each other with weapons ready, but the Sioux withdrew and a fight was avoided.

The expedition wintered with Mandan Indians in what is now central North Dakota, being forced to lay up there for five months in a fort they built and named Fort Mandan. It was there that they met the French fur trader Toussaint Charbonneau and his Shoshone wife, Sacajawea. The two agreed to join the expedition as guides and interpreters.

Sacajawea, referred to in the journals of both Lewis and Clark only as "the Indian woman" because neither of them could spell her name, was pregnant, and in February, she gave birth to a son. In April, the expedition was at last able to get underway once more. They reached the Great Falls of the Missouri River in June and in July the foothills of the Rocky Mountains.

They soon found themselves in Shoshone country, where a remarkable occurrence took place. They encountered a band of Shoshone hunters, whose first reaction was to get away from them. Then, the Shoshones recognized Sacajawea. The leader of the band was none other than her brother, Cameahwait. Since the corps had been forced to abandon its boats, the Shoshones provided them with horses.

The corps moved out again in late August, Sacajawea and her family still in their company. Along the way, they met the Nez Percés and admired their Appaloosa horses. They met the Chinooks and the Clatsops and other tribes, and on November 7, 1805, they finally arrived at the Pacific Ocean. They built Fort Clatsop there on what is now the border between Washington and Oregon, and they spent the winter of 1805–1806 there.

An undated, romanticized painting depicting Sacajawea guiding the Lewis and Clark expedition.

On the return trip, the party split into two groups. One, led by Clark, explored the Yellowstone River. The other, headed by Lewis, explored the Marias River. Lewis's group engaged in the expedition's first open conflict with Indians, killing two Blackfeet. The two groups met and rejoined where the Yellowstone and Missouri Rivers come together and for the rest of the return trip traveled together.

They reached St. Louis, Missouri, on September 23, 1806. They had been gone for twenty-eight months and traveled 7,689 miles (12,379 kilometers) at a cost of $38,722.22—considerably more than Jefferson's initial estimate. They brought back with them over a dozen notebooks filled with information on the western tribes and on the animals, plants, and the geography and climate of the region, as well as the first maps of the area. They had collected hundreds of plant and animal specimens, and they had made the first official contact between the United States and over fifty western Indian tribes.

Even while Lewis and Clark were still on their expedition, three different delegations of western tribes traveled to Washington to meet with President Thomas Jefferson, using their peace medals as passports. Others would follow. In the opposite direction, Lewis and Clark were followed by numerous "mountain men" moving into the "new territory" to hunt, trap, and engage in trade with the Indians.

— R. J. Conley

SEE ALSO:
Hudson's Bay Company; Louisiana Purchase; Sacajawea.

LEWIS, ANNA (1885–1961)

Anna Lewis, a Choctaw, was a distinguished Native American historian who was born in the Choctaw Nation in 1885. She began her schooling at the

on the bluffs overlooking the Little Bighorn. It was here that the seven companies held their defenses throughout the day and most of the next. The siege ended when the Indians withdrew upon the approach of the troops led by Terry and Gibbon.

During the battle, the Seventh Cavalry lost the five companies—C, E, F, I, and L—totaling casualties of 225 men with George Armstrong Custer among them. The other companies led by Reno and Benteen lost 47 men, and 52 were wounded. The Indian casualties are estimated at 60 to 100.

— T. Midge

SEE ALSO:

Black Hills; Cheyenne; Crazy Horse; Crazy Horse Memorial; Crook, George; Custer, George Armstrong; Fort Laramie Treaty of 1868; Gall; Little Bighorn Battlefield Monument; Siouan Nations.

SUGGESTED READINGS:

Axelrod, Alan. *Chronicle of the Indian Wars: From Colonial Times to Wounded Knee.* New York: Prentice Hall General Reference, 1993.

Ballantine, Betty, and Ian Ballantine. *The Native Americans: An Illustrated History.* Atlanta: Turner Publishing, Inc., 1993.

Brown, Dee. *Bury My Heart at Wounded Knee.* New York: Bantam Books, 1970.

Jennison, Keith, and John Tebbel. *The American Indian Wars.* New York: Bonanza Books, 1977.

Josephy, Alvin M., Jr. *500 Nations: An Illustrated History of North American Indians.* New York: Alfred A. Knopf, 1994.

Welch, James, and Paul Stekler. *Killing Custer.* New York: Penguin Books, 1995.

LITTLE BIGHORN BATTLEFIELD MONUMENT

The Little Bighorn Battlefield Monument has often been described as the only national battlefield monument in America named for the loser. This refers to the monument's original name, the Custer Battlefield National Monument. A 1991 congressional vote changed the name to what it is today. For over a century, the monument, erected in the 1880s, has paid homage to the defeat of the cavalry commanded by Lieutenant Colonel George Armstrong Custer on June 25, 1876. For Native people, however, the Little Bighorn Battlefield Monument memorializes one of the last armed efforts of the Plains Indians to preserve their ancestral way of life.

The monument lies within the Crow Indian Reservation in southeastern Montana and is administered by the National Park Service of the U.S. Department of the Interior. Located within the park area is a visitors' center, museum, national cemetery, and a stretch of rolling grass scattered with grave markings—the battlefield where U.S. soldiers fell. Near the visitors' center is Custer Hill, where a tall grave marker enclosed by a high fence marks the spot of the Battle of the Little Bighorn, popularly known as "Custer's Last Stand."

The battlefield tour begins at the Reno-Benteen battlesite, 4.5 miles (7.2 kilometers) from the park visitor center. It was at Reno-Benteen that Major Marcus Reno, leading three companies of Custer's divided command, attacked the Native village lying in the valley. Custer's Lookout is the site where Custer watched Reno's attack underway in the valley. It was here that Custer first saw a portion of the enormous Indian village that numbered between seven and ten thousand people, of whom two thousand were warriors. Weir Point is the site where Captain Thomas Weir led his company in the late afternoon of June 25. Medicine Tail Ford marks the Little Bighorn River's low banks, where part of Custer's battalion attempted to cross into the Indian village. Other sites on the tour include Calhoun Ridge and Calhoun Hill.

On June 28, 1876, the bodies of Custer and his men were buried at or near the places they fell. These shallow graves were improved in the next few years. Then, in 1881, those graves that could be found were reopened, and the bones were placed in a common grave around the base of the memorial shaft bearing the names of the soldiers killed in the battle. Custer's remains were reburied at the U.S. Military Academy, West Point, New York, on October 10, 1877.

The Battle of the Little Bighorn continues to fascinate people around the world. For some, it has come to illustrate a part of what Americans know as their western heritage. Heroism and suffering, humiliation and victory, and triumph and tragedy

Aerial view of the Little Bighorn Battlefield National Monument in Montana. In 1991, Congress changed the name of the monument from the Custer Battlefield National Monument.

are some of the conflicting fortunes that tourists come to the battle site to ponder.

For Native people, however, the monument means very different things. Conspicuously absent are markings or monuments paying homage to the several thousand Indians who were present during the battle and who rode away victorious. Nor are there grave markings for the estimated sixty to one hundred Indian warriors who died protecting their families and way of life. Plans have been made, however, to erect a permanent monument recognizing the Native people involved in the Battle of Little Bighorn.

SEE ALSO:
Cheyenne; Crazy Horse; Crazy Horse Memorial; Custer, George Armstrong; Fort Laramie Treaty of 1868; Gall; Siouan Nations.

LITTLE CROW (c. 1810–1863)

Little Crow was a hereditary chief of the Mdewakanton Santee Sioux. He was born in the village of Kapoosa on the upper Mississippi River. As an adult, he lived in a village that was located at the site of present-day St. Paul, Minnesota.

In 1851, Little Crow signed the Treaty of Mendota, in which the Santees were guaranteed an annual annuity and a reservation on the upper Minnesota River in exchange for much of their land. In 1857, he led a force of Sioux against another Sioux leader, Inkpaduta, whose band had killed some whites at Spirit Lake, Minnesota. The next year, Little Crow was part of the Sioux delegation that visited Washington, D.C.

Little Crow's friendly relations with the United States ended in 1862, when corrupt government officials brought the Santees to the brink of starvation by stealing their annuities. In what historians have called the Sioux Minnesota Uprising of 1862, Little Crow and other Sioux leaders waged a war in which hundreds of whites and Indians were killed. The government hanged a number of Sioux leaders, but Little Crow was able to withdraw with many of his people into Canada and Dakota territory.

Little Crow was shot and killed on July 3, 1863, near Hutchinson, Minnesota, while leading an expedition to try to replenish the Santee horse herd. The farmer who shot him was paid a bounty for his scalp. Little Crow's body was acquired by the Minnesota Historical Society, which put it on public display. In 1971, his remains were returned to his relatives, and a burial ceremony was held at a Sioux cemetery near Flandreau, South Dakota.

SEE ALSO:
Sioux Uprising (1862).

LOGAN, JOHN (c. 1725–1780)

John Logan, who was also known as James Logan, Logan the Mingo, Tachnechdorus, and Tahgahjute, became the principal leader of the Cayugas of the Iroquois Confederacy who had moved from upstate New York to the headwaters of the Ohio River in what is now western Pennsylvania. His mother was a Cayuga woman, and his father, Shikellamy, was French and had been raised by the Oneidas. Shikellamy was chosen by the Iroquois council as its representative for Iroquois holdings in western Pennsylvania. He moved to Shamokin, Pennsylvania, with his family, near the Susquehanna River, where his son, who would later call himself John Logan, was born about 1725.

Logan took his name from his English friend, John Logan, who at various times served as both secretary and acting governor of colonial Pennsylvania. The Cayugas who moved to western Pennsylvania became known as Mingos, and Logan succeeded his father as their principal leader. For many years, he lived near Reedsville, Pennsylvania, where he was known as a friend of white farmers in the area. He moved to the Ohio River about

1700, and by 1774, he was living at Old Chillicothe in present-day southeastern Ohio.

In the spring of 1774, a group of intruders entered the Ohio River Valley from the English colony of Virginia, in violation of the Proclamation of 1763, by which the king of England had ordered the English colonists not to cross the Appalachian Mountains into the Indian lands. The Virginia intruders, led by Jacob Greathouse, apparently thinking that they could lay claim to some Ohio River Valley land by killing the Indians in the immediate vicinity, fell upon a family of Mingos and massacred them. Among the dead were Logan's sister and other relatives. Logan, outraged and infuriated, launched reprisal attacks against the whites who had been intruding into the region. A frenzied alarm was sounded by the commander of Fort Pitt, and so began what became known as Lord Dunmore's War, which soon involved the Shawnees. In that war, colonial armies from Virginia forced the Shawnees to give up their claims to Kentucky.

After the war, Logan refused to participate in the peace talks. He fell victim to the ravages of alcohol, and the remainder of his life was undistinguished. He was killed in an argument with a nephew while returning home from a trip to Detroit in 1780.

SEE ALSO:
Lord Dunmore's War; Proclamation of 1763.

LONE WOLF (c. 1820–1879)

Lone Wolf, also known as Guipago, became the Kiowa principal chief at a great council of the Kiowas in 1866, when he was about forty-six years old. Eventually, he became a bitter antagonist of the United States and was one of the last Kiowa leaders to surrender at the end of the last Indian war on the southern Great Plains. He is thought to have been born about 1820, though very little is known about his early life. Lone Wolf was regarded by the Kiowas as possessing considerable medicine power. During a violent electrical storm on the plains, a lightning bolt had struck his tipi, killing his wife and child but leaving him unharmed.

Kiowa leader Lone Wolf, photographed by William S. Soule sometime between 1868 and 1874.

Lone Wolf made two trips to Washington, D.C., one in 1863 and one in 1872, but he remained unimpressed by the military and industrial power of the United States. Early in his career, however, he attempted to negotiate in good faith with the United States. He was chosen principal chief of the Kiowas in a compromise to try to maintain harmony within the nation between a war faction led by Santana and a peace faction led by Kicking Bird, but the nation was so deeply divided between these two factions that unified leadership proved to be impossible.

Lone Wolf signed the Medicine Lodge Treaty of 1867, which established boundaries for a Kiowa reservation in Indian Territory (present-day Oklahoma). Later, when he and other Kiowa leaders went to the camp of General Philip Sheridan under a white flag of truce to discuss the settlement of the Kiowas, they were arrested by Lieutenant Colonel George Custer and held as hostages until all of the Kiowas agreed to assemble at the Fort Cobb Agency in Indian Territory.

Already embittered by this experience, Lone Wolf was further alienated from the U.S. government when, in 1873, a party of raiding Texas federal troops killed his son and nephew. Lone Wolf led a large force of Kiowas south to avenge their deaths. The Kiowas had many other grievances against the United States, including the ongoing wanton slaughter of the southern buffalo herds by U.S. commercial buffalo hunters. Lone Wolf joined with Quanah Parker and the Comanches for an unsuccessful attack on an outpost of the commercial buffalo hunters at Adobe Walls in the present-day Texas panhandle. In August of 1874, his Kiowa forces fought the United States Army to a standstill at the Wichita Agency in Indian Territory. In September of 1874, however, the U.S. Army trapped practically the entire horse herd of the Kiowas and Comanches in Palo Duro Canyon (also in the present-day Texas panhandle) and killed nearly all of the horses. This loss forced Lone Wolf and all of the other Kiowas and Comanches to surrender at Fort Sill in the spring of 1875.

Along with about seventy-five other Kiowas, he was sent to prison at Fort Marion, Florida. He was confined there for three years, where he contracted malaria. He was released in May of 1878 and returned to Fort Sill, but he died within a year of his return. He was buried on Mt. Scott, overlooking the Fort Sill military post and the surrounding high plains country. His adopted son, also known as Lone Wolf, succeeded him as the principal leader of the nation. At the turn of the century, the younger Lone Wolf unsuccessfully contested in federal court the forced Congressional allotment of Kiowa reservation land to individual Kiowas and the opening up of the remaining land to Euro-American settlement.

SEE ALSO:

Comanche; General Allotment Act; Kicking Bird; Kiowa; *Lone Wolf v. Hitchcock*; Oklahoma; Parker, Quanah.

LONE WOLF V. HITCHCOCK

In the 1890s, the Kiowa warrior Lone Wolf (Mamay-day-te) (son of the late Kiowa principal chief, also named Lone Wolf) emerged as a leader of the opposition against the federal government's allotment of the Kiowa, Comanche, and Plains Apache (KCA) Reservation in western Oklahoma to individual settlers. The threatened opening of the KCA Reservation in 1901 led Lone Wolf to seek judicial relief to prevent Interior Secretary Ethan Allen Hitchcock from allotting reservation lands to Indians and opening the remaining lands to Anglo-American settlers.

Attorneys for Lone Wolf argued two major points: that the impending opening of the reservation lands was in violation of solemn pledges made in the 1867 Treaty of Medicine Lodge and that the remaining land left for tribespeople would be insufficient to support them. The federal government's counsel argued in favor of opening the lands to allotment. He stated that the federal government possessed paramount authority over Indians as wards under the care of the government. The Kiowas, and other Indians as well, had no choice but to comply with United States Indian policy.

After nearly a year of legal maneuvering in lower courts, the United States Supreme Court agreed to hear the case since it involved Indian treaty and land rights. On January 5, 1903, Justice Edward Douglas White read the opinion of the high court in the case of *Lone Wolf v. Hitchcock*. Justice White drew from earlier court rulings and ruled in favor of the federal government, giving it the authority to open the Indians' lands.

White underscored Congressional political power over the destiny of the Indians, writing that "full administrative power was possessed by Congress over Indian tribal property." Justice White also noted in his opinion that such power was political—that is, derived from Congress. The power, therefore, was not subject to legal review or control from the judicial branch of the federal government. Indian treaties could not limit Congressional guardianship over Indian property because Congress could "abrogate [abolish] the provisions of an Indian treaty" at any time.

This decision climaxed nineteenth-century federal intrusions into Indian sovereignty and pushed Indian self-government down to its lowest point. The decree crushed opponents of allotment, while it gave new power to those who wanted Indians forcibly assimilated into U.S. society. Despite his reputation as a military warrior, Lone Wolf could not hold off the legal decision that brought final defeat for his efforts. Indian landholdings decreased significantly in the years following the decree. The court's decree had even farther-reaching significance as U.S. military and civilian officials applied the ruling to U.S. overseas possessions that were acquired in the brief Spanish-American War, which had concluded at nearly the same time as the court decision.

SEE ALSO:
Dawes Commission; General Allotment Act; Kiowa; Indian Policy, U.S.; Lone Wolf; Oklahoma; Tribal Sovereignty.

LONG WALK, NAVAJO

The Navajo Long Walk occurred at the conclusion of a war waged against Navajos by the United States government in 1863–1864. More than eight thousand Navajos were forced to walk nearly 400 miles (640 kilometers), from their homeland in present-day northeastern Arizona and northwestern New Mexico to present-day east-central New Mexico.

Their destination was a concentration camp known as Bosque Redondo near Fort Sumner on the Pecos River. The Navajos were held at Bosque Redondo as prisoners of war for four years, eventually being allowed to return to their homeland in the summer of 1868.

In 1863–1864, the United States pursued a scorched earth policy throughout the Navajo Nation by burning crops, destroying hogans, chopping down orchards, and confiscating or killing large herds of sheep and horses. The policy was intended to starve the Navajos into surrendering. At the same time that U.S. Army troops, under the command of Colonel Kit Carson, were moving through the nation destroying its means of livelihood, bands of Utes from the north and vigilante groups of Anglo-American and Hispanic-American New Mexicans were also roaming the Navajo Nation. They, too, were bent on destruction: stealing livestock, killing Navajos, and capturing and selling Navajos as servants for non-Native households in New Mexico. Thus, as winter arrived, the Navajos found themselves facing starvation as well as being pursued relentlessly by the slave raiders, who were operating with the approval and consent of the U.S. Army. Their only chance for survival was to surrender to the army, and they did so by the thousands.

The U.S. Army was overwhelmed by the large numbers of Navajo people who streamed into Fort Canby and Fort Wingate. By February 1864, nearly eight hundred had arrived at the forts, and by March, the number had swollen to twenty-five hundred. Large groups continued to arrive every day, until eventually the total number of Navajos needing to be fed exceeded eight thousand. General James H. Carleton, who had conceived of and ordered the policy of starving the Navajos into submission, had estimated their population at no more than five thousand, so the army was not prepared to deal with so many people.

General Carleton's plan for establishing United States authority in the Navajo homeland was to depopulate the region of Navajo people, march them to Bosque Redondo, intern them there long enough to force them to adopt agriculture and Christianity, and then relocate them, probably to Indian Territory in present-day Oklahoma. Accordingly, as soon as the Navajos surrendered at Fort

On August 17, 1978, participants in the Longest Walk gathered on the steps of the United States Capitol in Washington, D.C. The five-month walk, originating in San Francisco, California, called attention to pending federal legislation that would adversely affect Native peoples.

On August 18, 1978, the peaceful demonstrations in Washington, D.C., continue at the conclusion of the Longest Walk. The participants visited the U.S. Capitol, the Supreme Court, and the White House.

Two days after the July 25, 1978, rally, United States Representative Ronald Dellums had the rally document printed in the Congressional Record. Today, the Longest Walk is remembered as a peaceful exercise of freedom of speech and an event that was widely supported throughout Indian country. The support included the National Tribal Chairman's Association, a group that had opposed the 1972 Trail of Broken Treaties.

SEE ALSO:
Activism, Indian; American Indian Movement; Bureau of Indian Affairs; Fishing Rights; Self-determination; Self-determination Policy; Trail of Broken Treaties.

LONGHOUSE

The longhouse of the Northeast is usually associated with the Iroquois people, although other Native peoples have been known to use it in vary-

ing sizes and forms in early woodland communities. The longhouse was essentially a dwelling structure with an inner skeleton of peeled and lashed-together saplings. These were covered with layers of elm or birch bark, which were stitched or laced together like overlapping shingles on a roof and further held in place with an outer skeleton of saplings. Usually the bark was inside out so that the plant tissue dried like tough leather and provided a slick surface off of which rain, ice, or snow could drain. The double lapping or shingling of the bark eliminated any cracks or openings, and so these dwellings were extremely tight and windproof.

The average longhouse was from forty to one hundred feet (twelve to thirty meters) long with doors at either end and smoke holes evenly spaced along the top of the peaked roof. A corridor ran the length of the house, which was divided into chambers or cubicles for family units. Bunks for sleeping and shelves for storage lined the entire length of the longhouse.

SEE ALSO:
Chief Joseph; Nez Perce.

LORD DUNMORE'S WAR

Lord Dunmore's War, which was a war of conquest for Indian land, was fought in the upper Ohio River Valley in 1774. It was named for John Murray (Lord Dunmore), who was the fourth earl of Dunmore and the British royal governor of the colony of Virginia. The war was started by the British colonists of Virginia, who coveted Indian land west of the Appalachian Mountains but could not legally settle there because the king of England, in the Proclamation of 1763, had declared that all land west of the Appalachian Mountains was Indian land, and he had ordered all British subjects to stay east of the mountains. The colonists, who included many land speculators who hoped to get rich from trading in Indian land and who were on the eve of breaking away from England in the American Revolution, ignored the Proclamation of 1763 and illegally squatted on land west of the mountains, where they provoked the Indians into war.

The Indian nations most directly involved were the Shawnees and the Mingos. Mingo is the tribal name that has come to be associated with the Cayugas of the Iroquois Confederacy who had earlier moved from upstate New York to present-day western Pennsylvania. Though the Indians of the upper Ohio River Valley had many grievances against the illegal squatters from the British colonies, it was an act of violence committed against the family of a Mingo leader that started the war. On April 30, 1774, British squatters led by Jacob Greathouse, for no apparent reason, murdered the sister of Chief Logan, and other family members, on the Ohio River at Yellow Creek, fifty miles (eighty kilometers) down the river from Fort Pitt.

Chief John Logan, a mixed-blood Cayuga who was also known as James Logan or Tachnechdorus, had been a strong supporter of peace with the colonists, but now he moved quickly to avenge the murder of his family members. The commander of Fort Pitt, John Connolly, sounded a frantic and defiant alarm throughout the region, and the war began.

The Shawnees of present-day southern Ohio did most of the fighting, but they were soon faced with large colonial armies. Lord Dunmore and Colonel Adam Stephen led eleven hundred men from northern Virginia, and Colonel Andrew Lewis led thirteen hundred men from far western Virginia. A Shawnee army of about one thousand men met and almost defeated Colonel Lewis's army on the south bank of the Ohio River on October 9, 1774. In what became known as the Battle of Point Pleasant, the Shawnees, led by their principal chief, Cornstalk, and by their principal war chief, Pucksinwah, were close to routing the Virginians in a daylong battle, when they mistook a flanking maneuver by the colonists for the arrival of reinforcements, which the Shawnees knew were on the way. The colonial reinforcements, however, did not arrive until the next day, by which time the Shawnees had withdrawn across the Ohio River. The Shawnees lost valuable leaders at the Battle of Point Pleasant, including Pucksinwah, the father of Tecumseh, who would himself eventually prove to be a great Shawnee leader.

The colonial armies then threatened the main Shawnee villages at Chillicothe, which included large numbers of women and children, and the Shawnees had to agree to peace terms, which would include giving up their hunting grounds across the Ohio River in Kentucky. The treaty ending the war was not formally negotiated until the next year, at a conference at Fort Pitt, which lasted from September 12 to October 12, 1775, by which time the American Revolution had begun. As a new condition of the treaty, the Shawnees were required to remain neutral during that conflict, but after two years, they entered the war on the side of the British, aware that the rebelling colonists were the greater threat to their survival.

SEE ALSO:

American Revolution; Iroquois Confederacy; Logan, John; Proclamation of 1763; Shawnee; Tecumseh.

LOUIS, ADRIAN C. (1946–)

Adrian C. Louis is a poet and novelist whose many works detail the brutal and harsh realities confronting American Indian people of the past, the present, and the future. His poetry has been described as hard-edged realism that speaks with biting truths and bitter ironies.

Louis was born in 1946 in Lovelock, Nevada, and is an enrolled member of the Lovelock Paiute Indian Tribe. He is a graduate of Brown University, where he also earned an M.A. in creative writing. As well as writing poetry, he has also edited four tribal newspapers, such as the *Lakota Times*, which is the largest Indian newspaper in North America, and was twice nominated as Print Journalist of the Year by the National Indian Media Consortium. He was also a cofounder of the Native American Press Association.

He has published several collections of poetry, including *Fire Water World*, which was published in 1989 by West End Press and won the 1989 Book Award from the Poetry Center at San Francisco State University; *Among the Dog Eaters*, 1992, West End Press; *Blood Thirsty Savages*, 1994, Time Being Books; *Vortex of Indian Fevers*, 1995, Triquarterly Books/Northwestern University Press; and a novel, *Skins*, published by Crown in 1995.

Louis is the recipient of several awards and fellowships from the South Dakota Arts Council, the Bush Foundation, and the National Endowment for the Arts. Since 1984, he has been teaching English at Oglala Lakota College on the Pine Ridge Reservation of South Dakota.

This New Orleans, Louisiana, Mardi Gras participant is wearing elaborate regalia. Many of the costumes worn by Mardi Gras celebrants include the use of Native symbols and imagery.

LOUISIANA

Louisiana became the eighteenth U.S. state on April 30, 1812. Louisiana has a long history of Indian inhabitation, with archaeological sites that have been dated to 8000 B.C.E. The state also has sites from the Mound Builder culture that flourished nearly three thousand years ago. The great Poverty Point site was constructed at about 700 B.C.E. and is nearly a mile (1.6 kilometers) across.

When the first permanent European settlement was established in Natchitoches in 1714, six major tribes lived in Louisiana. The Caddo lived in the northwest, the Natchez in the middle of the state, the Atakapa in the southwest, the Chitimachan in the south, the Muskogean in the east, and the Tunican in the northeast. Each of these tribes existed by farming and by hunting and fishing, and each lived in villages of permanent dwellings. Some of the tribes may have been the descendants of the Mound Builders and liked to have their villages near mound sites. The Natchez, for example, had one of their primary villages near Emerald Mound. More is known of the Natchez than of some of the other tribes because early French settlers lived near the Natchez and chronicled their interesting social structure.

There were four social classes in Natchez culture. The lowest class were the Stinkards. The next class were the Honored Men. Above that were the Nobles, and highest of all were the Suns, with the Great Sun ruling over all. Within the culture, upper classes were required to marry someone from a lower class, so over time there was a great deal of social movement.

In 1729, the Natchez attacked the French and almost wiped out the Louisiana settlements. When the French regrouped, however, they took a terrible vengeance on the Natchez and almost completely eradicated the tribe.

During the late 1700s and the early 1800s, two other tribes moved into Louisiana. The Alabamas, who were part of the Creek Confederacy, moved into Louisiana in 1764, but in 1854, they moved into Texas. The Quapaw, or Arkansas, moved onto the Caddo Reservation in 1824, but they moved on to Indian Territory (present-day Oklahoma) in 1833. In 1835, the Caddos left Louisiana and moved into Texas, but Texan attacks caused the tribe to move north into Oklahoma in 1854.

Three very small reservations currently exist in Louisiana. The Chitimacha Reservation consists of 283 acres (113 hectares) and has 212 Indian residents. The Coushatta Reservation has 154 acres (62 hectares) and 33 residents. Smallest of all, the Tunica-Biloxi Reservation has just 134 acres (54 hectares) and 16 Indian residents. The 1990 U.S. Census lists 18,541 Louisiana residents as being Native American, ranking the state twenty-fourth in terms of Indian population.

SEE ALSO:
Caddo; Creek; France; Mound Builders; Quapaw; Removal Act, Indian.

LOUISIANA PURCHASE

The Louisiana Purchase has been dealt with in many history books as a land purchase and is therefore thought by many people to have been a major real estate deal. It was not, however, an outright purchase of land. The so-called Doctrine of Discovery the European powers had agreed upon gave the "discoverer" the exclusive right to negotiate with the Native populations for the purchase of their lands.

In other words, that land now known as the Louisiana Purchase never belonged to France, not even in the mind of the French government. When U.S. President Thomas Jefferson made his deal with Napoleon (the soon-to-be emperor of France), he bought from France the exclusive right to negotiate with the Native tribes for the land in the area under consideration. Nothing more.

The deal was made between the United States and France in 1803, when the U.S. paid France approximately $15 million dollars for its rights in an area of more than 800,000 square miles (2,080,000 square kilometers), an area that extended from the Mississippi River to the Rocky Mountains and from the Gulf of Mexico to the Canadian border. This area was larger than the entire United States at that time. By international law, the United States could not actually own any of the land unless and until it was acquired legally from the owners, the Indian tribes who lived on the land. Their title to the land was recognized in international law as "aboriginal title."

This vast territory was virtually unknown. Few Europeans had penetrated the area, and those who had, mostly Spanish gold seekers and French fur traders, knew the waterways primarily. There were outlandish tales of mountains made entirely of salt, tribes of Welsh-speaking Indians, eighteen-inch- (forty-six-centimeter-) tall devils, and man-hating Amazons.

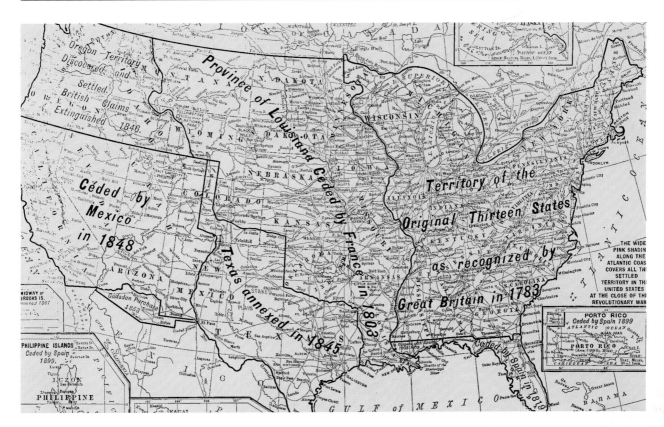

The French province of Louisiana consisted of an immense portion of the North American continent, including the northern Great Plains. This map shows the carving up of North America around the time of the Louisiana Purchase.

For that reason, President Jefferson commissioned the Lewis and Clark expedition, or the Corps of Discovery, to explore the region. The expedition began on May 14, 1804, and ended September 23, 1806. There were also two expeditions led by Zebulon Pike into what was then called the Louisiana Territory during the years 1805, 1806, and 1807. Almost immediately, American "mountain men" began moving into the area to hunt and trap, giving competition to those French "voyageurs" who had preceded them.

In spite of the legalities of the purchase, the United States immediately began acting as if it owned the land, for not only did it send the expeditions mentioned above and approve of the invading mountain men, it also began to make use of the Louisiana Territory as a place in which to shove eastern Indians. And it began to treat the area as a formal territory with a governor appointed by the president of the United States.

SEE ALSO:

France; Lewis and Clark Expedition.

LUCAS, PHIL

Phil Lucas is a Choctaw film director and founder of Phil Lucas Productions, Inc. The company develops projects for motion picture and television productions and produces independent films and videos.

Lucas earned a bachelor's degree in science and visual communication in 1970. From 1979 to 1981, he was the writer, codirector, and coproducer of a five-part Public Broadcasting Corporation series titled *Images of Indians*. These films examined the use of the stereotypes perpetuated in Hollywood productions about Native Americans. The series received a 1980 Special Achievement Award in Documentary Film from the American Indian Film Institute.

Lucas's productions provide accurate portraits of Native Americans. *Nez Perce: Portrait of People* (1982), is a twenty-minute color film depicting the history and culture of the Nez Perce Nation. In recent years, Lucas's professional vision has continued to strengthen with such films as *Circle of*

This movie poster glamorizes battles between Indians and non-Native Americans as "glorious." Phil Lucas examined similar Hollywood Indian stereotypes in his five-part PBS documentary, *Images of Indians*. Lucas was active in writing, directing, and producing the documentary.

Warriors (1989) and *Lookin' Good* (1988). Lucas has also produced films about drug and alcohol prevention and the AIDS virus. In the film *Where We've Been and Where We're Going* (1983), Lucas reports on the topic of alcoholism. And in the film *I'm Not Afraid of Me* (1990), he presents the story of a Native woman and her daughter, both of whom have AIDS.

In 1989, Lucas produced a fifteen-part series titled *Native Indians: Images of Reality*. This film, told from the point of view of Indian people, presents a portrait of the realities of Indian lives.

LUMBEE

The origins of the Lumbee Tribe of Cheraw Indians, as the nation is now known, are shrouded in mystery. Their homeland, in the southern reaches of present-day Robeson County, North Carolina, was isolated, with swamplands not coveted by whites, and the tribe escaped the clamor for Indian removal during the 1830s.

A Lumbee posing in traditional Native dress in Lumberton, North Carolina.

By the time they came to the attention of various state and federal authorities, they were heavily intermarried and had lost their native language but not their internal tribal identity and close-knit society. North Carolina legislatures struggled for more than a century attempting to classify them. In 1835, they were designated as "free people of color." In 1885, they were called "Croatan Indians." In 1911, they were called "Robeson County Indians." In 1913, they were called "Cherokee Indian of Robeson County." Finally, in 1953, the legislature adopted the use of the name the people themselves prefer, the Lumbees, when the state granted them official recognition as an Indian nation. In 1956, the federal government also granted them official recognition but denied them access to federal Indian services. Since that time, the Lumbees have attempted to gain access to those services, and in 1994 they succeeded in gaining Congressional approval in the U.S. House of Representatives only to see the measure defeated in the U.S. Senate.

There has been much speculation that the Lumbees may have absorbed the entire population of the English colonists who disappeared from the Roanoke Island colony in 1587. This would account for the high degree of mixed blood that has been present in the Lumbee population from an early date following the coming of European colonizers to North America. These speculations would trace Lumbee ancestry to the indigenous peoples who lived along Cape Hatteras, in present-day North Carolina, at the time of European contact.

Lumbees have produced many prominent leaders. Their greatest folk hero was named Henry Berry Lowry, who organized resistance to Confederate edicts for Lumbee forced labor during the Civil War. He also continued to fight against the Reconstructionist authorities who came into the South from the North after the war. He led daring raids against Confederate plantations during the war and opposed the racist policies of the Ku Klux Klan after the war. He was never captured, and no one knows when or how he died, which has only added to the legendary nature of his feats.

In 1875, the Lumbees sought and received state approval to organize their own school system, which operated for eighty years. They also maintained a school of higher education, which today is known as Pembroke State University. In 1958, the Lumbees gained national attention when they refused to allow the Ku Klux Klan to stage a major rally in a field in Robeson County. As Klan members gathered for the rally, so did the Lumbees, in large numbers. They routed the Klan from the field and drove them out of Robeson County, which has since refused to tolerate the Klan's return.

The strength of Lumbee social life can be found in more than one hundred churches in Robeson County whose memberships are restricted to members of the tribe. The churches are focal points for tribal community life and training grounds for leaders. The communities are tightly knit, and both the churches and communities hold annual homecoming celebrations that are highly attended by Lumbees who have left the area.

Most Lumbees remain in Robeson County, North Carolina. The tribe is one of the largest on the continent, with a 1990 U.S. Census count of 48,444. According to the census, the tribal members were concentrated in five states: 42,397 in North Carolina, 1,038 in Maryland (where many Lumbees have congregated in Baltimore), 652 in Michigan, 576 in Virginia, and 540 in South Carolina.

SEE ALSO:

Civil War, U.S., Indians in the; Removal Act, Indian; Roanoke Island Natives and Roanoke Colony.

LUMMI

Prior to European contact, the Lummi people, a Native nation of the Pacific Northwest, occupied the San Juan and other islands of Puget Sound as well as the adjacent mainland. They spoke a coastal dialect of Salishan. Their economy was based on sockeye salmon, which they caught using nets from their canoes and other water-based craft. The Lummis supplemented their diets by occasionally hunting beaver, muskrat, and bear and by gathering roots and berries. The Lummis were sedentary during the harsh winter months, gathering in groups of up to twenty longhouses, each housing one or more extended families. They spent the rest of the year fishing the Puget Sound islands. Leadership among the Lummis was based on wealth and family lineage, and social classes were composed of nobles, commoners, and slaves. The Lummis intermarried and traded with other tribes in their area.

In 1827, the Hudson's Bay Company set up a trading post in the area to capitalize on the region's natural resources. This initial incursion was followed in the 1850s by European settlers. The European presence diminished both the Lummi people and their land. The population was reduced by warfare and disease, and the land was lost to unscrupulous traders and to the U.S. government. The government originally assigned the Lummis to a reservation within their old territory. In 1886, however, the government decided to allot reservation land to individual tribe members. By the 1950s, it was estimated that only 60 percent of the allotted lands were still owned by tribal members.

The Lummi have, however, made a comeback. According to the 1990 census, their population has increased to almost three thousand. Although very

In 1827, the Hudson's Bay Company established a post near the Lummis. Here employees of the company are shown as they begin their annual trading expedition.

few tribal members still speak Salishan, there has been, with the reintroduction of traditional ceremonies, a cultural resurgence to match the population growth. The Lummis have also embarked on a pioneering self-government project that has essentially freed them of control by the Bureau of Indian Affairs. The tribal government has also initiated successful aquaculture projects, including raising salmon and harvesting oysters, clams, and berries along bodies of water.

SEE ALSO:

Bureau of Indian Affairs; General Allotment Act; Hudson's Bay Company.

Oren Lyons has become internationally known as a spokesperson for the Iroquois Confederacy. He has dealt with issues involving both Native and non-Native governance.

LYONS, OREN (JOAGQUISHO) (1931–)

Oren Lyons (Onondaga) became known worldwide during the last half of the twentieth century as a spokesperson for the Iroquois Grand Council at Onondaga, as well as an author, publisher, and crisis negotiator. Lyons was the lead author of the 1992 study of Native American constitutionalism, *Exiled in the Land of the Free: Democracy, Indian Nations, and the U.S. Constitution* (Santa Fe: Clear Light Publishers).

Lyons enjoyed a successful career as a commercial artist in New York City before returning home to Onondaga, New York, where he was selected as faithkeeper of the Iroquois Grand Council. He also edited the Native American newspaper *Daybreak*, published in the early 1990s. In addition, Lyons is an artist of note and a member of the Syracuse sports Hall of Fame for his activities as an All-American lacrosse player for Syracuse University in the 1950s. In 1990, Lyons organized an Iroquois national team that played in the world lacrosse championships in Australia.

Lyons also was part of a negotiating team from the Iroquois Confederacy that helped resolve the 1990 standoff between Mohawks and authorities at Kanesatake (Oka), Quebec. The Confederacy's negotiators occupied a crucial middle ground between the Mohwak warriors and Canadian officials during months of negotiations. These negotiations were able to avert the use of armed force by the Canadian Army and police at Kanesatake and Kahnawake. The Iroquois negotiators urged both sides to concentrate on long-term solutions to problems that had been brought to light by the summer's violence. They recommended a fair land-rights process, the creation of viable economic bases for the communities involved in the crisis, and the recognition of long-standing (but often ignored) treaty rights, including border rights.

SEE ALSO:

Iroquois Confederacy; Kahnawake Mohawks; Lacrosse.

A Maine Penobscot man in the early twentieth century. The Penobscots have long played a role in relations between Natives and Euro-Americans in New England.

MAINE

Maine became the twenty-third U.S. state on March 15, 1820. The state's name comes from fishermen working off the Maine coast who called the mainland "the main" in order to distinguish it from offshore islands.

Indian peoples have lived in Maine for a very long time. Some depended on the sea for much of their food; over time, great shell piles grew up as the Indians harvested that food source. Some of these shell piles are five thousand years old.

The first Europeans to visit Maine were the Vikings, who briefly had a settlement in Maine at about 1000 C.E. About six hundred years later, English and French groups attempted to seize land in Maine. The first permanent European settlement was begun in 1629. At that time, there were several

Indian tribes who called the area now known as Maine home. The Abenaki Confederacy was made up of five tribes: the Etchimin, the Malecite, the Passamaquoddy, the Penobscot, and the Sokoki. Of these tribes, the Penobscot was the largest. Early European visitors to Maine were so impressed with Penobscot villages that early maps labeled their territory a kingdom—the "Kingdom of Norumba." In addition to the Abenaki Confederacy were the Pennacook or Merrimac Indians, who lived in fortified villages and who were aligned with the Abenakis.

Both the Abenakis and the Pennacooks were in conflict with the Iroquois Confederacy and with the Iroquois's English allies. The Abenakis and Pennacooks fought as allies of the French. During

King Philip's War and during the French and Indian War, the Abenakis killed many English settlers in Maine. As the balance of power shifted to the English, the Abenakis and Pennacooks could see that the English would ultimately win. In 1749, the Penobscots made a treaty with the English; other Abenaki tribes moved north into Canada.

During the 1700s, much of the Indian land in Maine was seized. Two centuries later, in 1972, a suit was brought by the Passamaquoddy and Penobscot tribes to regain lost land. The suit was settled in 1980, and the tribes were awarded $81 million and 300,000 acres (120,000 hectares) of land.

Three reservations exist in Maine. Indian Township Reservation contains 23,000 acres (9,200 hectares) and 541 residents. The Penobscot Reservation is made up of 127,838 acres (51,135 hectares) and has 430 residents. Pleasant Point Reservation is small and contains only 200 acres (80 hectares),

although 523 Indians live there. The 1990 U.S. Census lists 5,998 Indians as residents of Maine, which ranks Maine forty-second among states in Native American population.

SEE ALSO:
Abenaki; French and Indian War; Iroquois Confederacy; King Philip's War; Passamaquoddy; Penobscot.

MAKAH

The Makah Reservation is located in Clallam County in Washington State; its tribal headquarters are in Neah Bay, Washington. The Makah Tribe has 1,600 enrolled members, with 940 living on-reservation, and the Makah Reservation contains 28,112 acres (112,448 hectares).

A view of the Ozette village site, now a memorial, and Tskawayah Island, a sacred Makah site, in the Cape Alava area of the North Olympic coast, Washington State.

Makah is a derivation of the Salish word *maq'a*, which means "generous with food." The tribe originally called itself *qwidicca a-tx*, which means "people who live on the cape by the rocks."

The Makah Nation is composed of five villages along the northwest coast of the Olympic Peninsula in Washington State: Wayatch, Neah Bay, Biheda, Tsoo-yess, and Ozette. The Makah people originally inhabited land that extended over a large portion of the Olympic Peninsula. The current reservation, around Cape Flattery, represents just a small portion of their former land.

Makah culture has remained traditional, and the Makah people have a special bond with their historical past. Around five hundred years ago, the Makahs were a hunting and fishing people, and their preferred prey consisted of gray whales and fur seals.

In 1969, the Makahs were given a view of this past when the remains of an ancient Makah village were discovered at Ozette. Thousands of artifacts dating back to the early fifteenth century were unearthed. The artifacts confirmed a highly developed technology in wood, bone, stone, and fibers. Many of the everyday artifacts contained symbolic artwork, and other items, such as storage boxes made from single planks, revealed superior carpentry.

In 1855, the Makah Tribe signed the Treaty of Neah Bay. At that time, the Makah were famous as fishers and hunters. They manufactured large amounts of whale and sea oil and sold these products to steamships and lumber operations. Makah halibut and smoked salmon were shipped as far away as China.

In the early part of the twentieth century, the Makah also made great profits from lumber sales. Many Makah worked in the lumber mills for companies such as Washington Pulp and Crown Zallerbach until the old growth lumber was all cut down.

In 1934, the Makah Tribe accepted the terms of the Wheeler-Howard Indian Reorganization Act (also known as the Indian New Deal), which allowed Indian tribes to form their own tribal governments. In 1936, the Makah Tribe approved a constitution that established a five-member tribal council. The members of the tribal council serve in staggered three-year terms. Today, the Makah Tribe has fishing rights and is a member of the Northwest Indian Fisheries Commission.

In the winter of 1804–1805, the Lewis and Clark expedition spent five months with Mandan Indians in present-day North Dakota. There, they would meet Sacajawea, a Shoshone, and her French husband, who joined the expedition as guides and interpreters.

SEE ALSO:

Indian New Deal (Indian Reorganization Act); Washington Coast and Puget Sound Indians, History of; Washington State.

MANDAN

The Mandans are a Siouan-speaking people of the northern Great Plains. They are known to have migrated to the Great Plains from the Ohio River Valley in the early fifteenth century. They settled first along the Missouri River near the mouth of the White River in present-day South Dakota. They moved upriver to an area known as the Big Bend of the Missouri, near the mouth of the Heart River in present-day North Dakota. There they came into contact with Europeans and later with citizens of the United States.

The Mandans established permanent villages, practicing agriculture and supplementing their diets by hunting buffalo. Their traditional houses dur-

A nineteenth-century illustration of a group of Mandans participating in a ceremonial dance. A devastating small-pox epidemic and a series of U.S. legislative acts reduced the size of the Mandan community in the 1800s. In 1954, a reservoir project by the U.S. Army Corps of Engineers further reduced the size of the land shared by Mandans, Hidatsas, and Arikaras.

ing this time consisted of large earth lodges that accommodated up to sixty people. In times of extremely harsh weather, there was even room inside the lodges for horses. The lodges were dug into the earth, sometimes as deep as four feet (1.2 meters). A sturdy wooden frame was then covered with large strips of sod from the prairie. Thus insulated, the lodges provided warm homes during winter blizzards and were cool in the hot summers. The roofs of the structures were so sturdy that large numbers of people were able to sit on top of them, which they frequently did in the summertime.

The Mandans were visited by the Lewis and Clark expedition of 1804. During the 1830s, they were painted by George Catlin and Karl Bodmer. In 1837, the American Fur Company established Fort Clark near the Mandan villages. Within a few months of the establishment of the fort, a devastating smallpox epidemic broke out among the Mandans. Their population had been estimated at about 9,000 in the middle of the eighteenth century. After the smallpox epidemic, fewer than 250 of them, and possibly as few as 125, were left alive.

In 1845, the Mandans moved with a neighboring tribe, the Hidatsas, to Fort Berthold in western North Dakota. In 1862, the Arikaras also moved to Fort Berthold. In 1871, a permanent reservation was established for these three tribes at that location. Today, they are formally known as the Three Affiliated Tribes. They work together when dealing with state and federal agencies while maintaining their own separate tribal identities and cultures within the reservation.

Today, the reservation consists of about nine hundred thousand acres (360,000 hectares), with more than half of it owned by non-Indians. Enrollment in the Three Affiliated Tribes is about six thousand, with about half of the people living off of the reservation. Jobs in federal and tribal agencies on the reservation provide most of the employment opportunities. The unemployment rate is high. In 1993, the tribes opened a high-stakes gambling casino, which has provided more jobs for tribal members.

The summer months are a busy time for cultural activities, including frequent powwows, which are sponsored by most communities on the reservation. Finely crafted items of beadwork and quillwork are sold at a tribal tourist complex and at fairs and powwows. The tribes also maintain a museum.

SEE ALSO:

American Fur Company, The; Arikara; Hidatsa; Lewis and Clark Expedition; Siouan Nations.

MANIFEST DESTINY

Manifest Destiny was a powerful idea that became a rationale for aggression and for the conquest of territory by the United States in the nineteenth century. It was both a religious and a political belief. The essence of the belief was that a supernatural being had ordained that it was the destiny of the United States to expand its territory all the way across the North American continent, from the Atlantic Ocean to the Pacific Ocean. This idea had no regard for the rights of the indigenous peoples of the continent. Under the powerful grip of

this idea, the citizens of the United States convinced themselves that they were not committing acts of aggression when they seized Indian lands, but that they were merely fulfilling their "destiny" to rule the continent. The idea is still alive today, as many American historians attempt to justify the conquest of the continent, especially in texts written for schoolchildren.

"Manifest" means self-evident. It was not always self-evident that the United States would even survive as a nation, let alone spread across the continent. During the early years of the republic, its survival within the reach of powerful European armies and navies was an open question, and one that greatly concerned the first leaders of the nation. The United States was so weak, compared to the European powers, that when British naval vessels stopped U.S. sailing vessels on the high seas and forced U.S. citizens to leave their ships and serve in the British Navy (a practice called impressment), President Thomas Jefferson closed all American ports and forced American ships to remain at anchor rather than risk war with England over the

A Native observer watches the celebration from a distance as the last spike of the transcontinental railroad is driven home in Utah in 1869. Propelled by the view that it was the "Manifest Destiny" of the United States to extend its reach across the entire continent, non-Native Americans eagerly carved a web of tracks, roads, paths, and settlements through Indian lands.

Wilma Mankiller, then-principal chief of the Cherokee Nation of Oklahoma, is shown at a 1988 White House meeting between President Ronald Reagan and several Indian leaders. Since her tenure as principal chief ended in 1994, Mankiller has continued to be a popular and respected voice on many issues of concern to all Americans.

in 1957, her family moved to San Francisco under a federal relocation program designed to encourage Indian people to move to urban areas.

Inspired by her father's activist attitudes, Mankiller became politically active herself in San Francisco. She became involved in Indian-rights issues through the San Francisco Indian Center and in 1969 joined in the activist takeover of Alcatraz Island as a way of dramatizing the position that unused federal land should be returned to Native Americans.

In 1976, Mankiller moved back to Oklahoma with her daughters, where she began working with the Cherokee Nation of Oklahoma to improve the living conditions of tribal members by, among other things, helping people put in their own water sys-

tems. In 1979, she was in a serious car accident and soon after she learned that she had a muscular disease caused by a nerve disorder. The effects of this condition and the medicine she was taking would lead to her having a kidney transplant in 1990. Her brother Louis Donald Mankiller donated one of his kidneys for the operation.

In 1983, Mankiller was elected to the position of deputy chief of the Cherokee Nation of Oklahoma, and in 1985, she became the first woman to serve as principal chief of the Cherokee Nation when Principal Chief Ross Swimmer resigned that position to take a job in Washington, D.C. In 1987, she was elected to the position and named Woman of the Year by *Ms.* magazine. Mankiller was reelected in 1991, and by the time she served out her tenure as principal chief in 1994, she had carved out a place for herself as one of the most influential chiefs in Cherokee Nation history. In 1990, she signed an agreement with the federal government granting the Cherokee Nation the right to self-governance, and in addition to helping bring much-needed programs and services to the Cherokee people, Mankiller won respect and admiration for her leadership role among Natives and non-Natives alike. As a past principal chief, Mankiller has continued working with the Cherokee Nation and has become a highly sought-after public speaker on issues of concern to Indians and women.

In 1993, her autobiography, *Mankiller: A Chief and Her People*, which she coauthored with Michael Wallis, was published and became a best-seller.

SEE ALSO:

American Indian Movement; Cherokee; Cherokee Literature, Contemporary.

MANUELITO (c. 1818–1894)

Manuelito was a prominent Navajo leader during the second half of the 1800s when the Navajos struggled to adjust to the intrusion of the United States into their homeland and their lives following the end of the Mexican-American War in 1848. He was born in present-day southeastern Utah, probably near Bear's Ear Peak in about 1818.

By 1855, he had succeeded Zarcillas Largas as headman of his band. In that year, the United States built Fort Defiance, near Canyon de Chelly, in the heart of the Navajo homeland, which greatly increased friction between the Navajos and the United States Army. In 1858, the commander of the fort demanded the use of Navajo grazing lands near the fort. When the Navajos refused to give up the use of these grazing lands, the U.S. Army shot the Navajo livestock on the range, including more than one hundred sheep and sixty horses belonging to Manuelito. Warfare broke out between the Navajos and the United States.

In 1860, Manuelito was one of the leaders of a large force of Navajos and other Indians that almost succeeded in capturing the fort. In 1863, the U.S. Army began a scorched earth campaign to destroy Navajo homes, crops, and livestock and starve them into submission. By the spring of 1864, thousands of starving Navajos had surrendered and were marched to eastern New Mexico for internment in a concentration camp at Bosque Redondo.

Manuelito and his followers were among the last Navajos to surrender, in September of 1866. They, too, were sent to Bosque Redondo. From there, Manuelito was a member of the Navajo delegation that visited Washington, D.C., to try to negotiate a settlement. On June 1, 1868, he was one of the Navajos who signed the agreement at Fort Sumner that allowed the Navajos to return to their homeland. He was also one of the leaders

Noted Navajo leader Manuelito sits for a photographic portrait taken sometime during his tenure as chief from 1855 to 1872, when he became head of a Navajo police force.

who led the march of approximately seven thousand Navajos back to their homes.

Manuelito represented his people on two more trips to Washington, D.C., and in 1872, he became commander of a newly organized Navajo police force. In 1893, he traveled to the Chicago World's Fair. He died in 1894 from measles and pneumonia.

SEE ALSO:

Bosque Redondo; Canyon de Chelly; Mexican-American War; Navajo.

MARKOOSIE PATSANG (1942–)

Born in 1942, Markoosie Patsang is a Canadian Inuit who lives deep within the Arctic Circle at Resolute Bay. In addition to being a novelist, Markoosie is also an Arctic pilot, the first Canadian Inuit to gain a commercial flying license. Markoosie's novel, *Harpoon of the Hunter*, first appeared in the newsletter *Inuttituut*, published by the Cultural Development Division of the Department of Indian Affairs and Northern Development in Canada.

Harpoon of the Hunter, which was published in 1970, tells the story of sixteen-year-old Kamik, who goes with his father and almost all of the hunters from their small camp to hunt a rabid bear that has attacked the camp. Kamik faces terrible ordeals in the novel, and all of the novel's major characters are dead by the novel's end. The novel was first written and published in Inuit in syllabics (a form of verse based on the number of syllables in a line) and later translated by Markoosie for publication in English. It is the first long work of Inuit fiction to be published in English.

SEE ALSO:
Inuit.

MARTINEZ, MARIA MONTOYA (1887–1980)

Maria Martinez became the most famous twentieth-century Pueblo potter. She was born April 5, 1887, in the Tewa-speaking pueblo of San Ildefonso in New Mexico. As a child, she learned

In this undated photo, Maria Montoya Martinez and her husband, Julian Martinez, are surrounded by their work at San Ildefonso Pueblo, New Mexico. During the long course of her career, Maria Montoya Martinez collaborated in her craft with various members of her family, winning honor and respect from several generations of admirers.

to make pottery from her aunt, Nicolasa Montoya, who was a noted Pueblo potter. In 1904, Maria first demonstrated Pueblo pottery making at the St. Louis World's Fair, the first of three world's fairs where she would demonstrate her craft.

The trip to St. Louis was her honeymoon. Until his death in 1943, her husband, Julian Martinez, collaborated with her in creating pottery. Maria produced the vessels, shaping and polishing them. Julian painted them, and then together they fired the vessels in a kiln.

In 1907, Julian worked at an excavation of Pueblo ruins. Edgar Hewett, who was directing the excavation, asked Maria if she would try to re-create an ancient form of pottery based on potsherds from the site. The ancient pottery was more highly polished and was thinner and harder than the contemporary pottery of the pueblo. After repeated experimentation, she succeeded in duplicating the ancient pottery.

In 1911, she and her husband began demonstrating pottery at the Museum of New Mexico at Santa Fe. They developed a technique for making black on black pottery by 1919. In 1923, Maria began signing her pottery, which by that time was in high demand by collectors.

After the death of her husband in 1943, Maria collaborated with her daughter-in-law, Santana. In 1956, she began collaborating with her son Tony, who is known as Popovi Da. Many other members of the family have also achieved distinction in the craft in recent years.

Maria Montoya Martinez's pottery won many awards during her life. She received honorary doctoral degrees and was invited to the White House four times. She died on July 20, 1980, at San Ildefonso Pueblo.

Dressed in beaded buckskin, a Piscataway dancer participates in an intertribal event. Along with the Nanticokes, the Pocomoke-Assateagues, and the Susquehannas, the Piscataways were one of the first Native peoples encountered by early European colonists in Maryland during the 1600s.

SEE ALSO:
Pueblo; Tewa Pueblo.

MARYLAND

Maryland became the seventh U.S. state on April 28, 1788. The state was probably named for Henrietta Maria, the queen of England and wife to Charles I, but Spanish explorers who visited Chesapeake Bay in the early 1500s also called the area Santa Maria.

Before the first Europeans arrived in Maryland, American Indians had been living in the area for thousands of years. Captain John Smith visited Maryland in 1608, and William Claiborne established the first permanent European settlement in what would become Maryland in 1631. At the time Claiborne began his settlement, there were four Indian tribes living in the state. The Piscataways lived on the Western Shore of Maryland, and the Nanticokes and the Pocomoke-Assateagues lived on the Eastern Shore along with Susquehannas, or Susquehannocks. The Susquehannas lived in permanent villages during most of the year, but in the summer, they lived in temporary sites on the seacoast, where they fished and collected shellfish.

The Susquehannas were nearly wiped out during a war with the Iroquois Confederacy, and for a period of time, the remaining members of the tribe lived in captivity with the Oneidas. Eventually, the Oneidas allowed the Susquehannas to return to their homelands, but English pressure caused the tribe to move westward into Pennsylvania. The other tribes in Maryland were also forced to move westward because of European aggression.

Maryland contains no federal Indian reservations. The National Museum of the American Indian, which was established by the United States Congress in 1989, does maintain a research facility in Maryland, however. The 1990 U.S. Census lists 12,972 Native residents, ranking the state thirty-first in Native American population.

SEE ALSO:
Iroquois Confederacy; Oneida.

MASAYESVA, VICTOR, JR.

Victor Masayesva, Jr., is a Hopi filmmaker from Hotevilla, a village of about five hundred people on Third Mesa in the Hopi Nation, which is located in northeastern Arizona. At a Native American film festival at the University of Oklahoma, Masayesva said that he had never been to a town larger than Winslow, Arizona, until he went to New York City at age fifteen. He studied still photography at Princeton University and then began working with video. He is an active participant and leader in the Native American Producers Association and in ATLATL, a national service organization for Native American artists. He is also curator of the Native American Film and Video Festival at the Scottsdale Center for the Arts in Scottsdale, Arizona.

Masayesva is the producer and director of a feature-length film entitled *Imagining Indians*. Part movie and part documentary, this ninety-minute film explores many facets of what happens when Native stories, rituals, and objects become commercial commodities. Clips of Hollywood classics depicting Indians blend with interviews with Native extras and crew members from the sets of *Dances with Wolves* and *Thunderheart*, with clips of Hopi people vigorously debating whether or not to allow a movie called *Dark Wind* to be filmed on Hopi land, with Anglo collectors of Indian artifacts, and with many other clips and interviews, some hilariously funny, some sad, all presented against the backdrop of a Native woman visiting an Anglo dentist and listening, while he drills her teeth, to his scheme to get rich by investing in New Age weekend seminars that will teach wealthy non-Natives how to gain Native spirituality.

Masayesva has screened *Imagining Indians* in Phoenix, Arizona; Santa Fe, New Mexico; Houston, Texas; Boston, Massachusetts; and New York City. The film received an enthusiastic reception at a screening before an audience predominantly composed of Native Americans at the 1994 Native American Film Festival at the University of Oklahoma. A sixty-minute version has been edited for television.

At the film festival at the University of Oklahoma, Masayesva said that he is now having second thoughts about one of his earlier films, *Ritual Clowns*, and is thinking about taking it out of distribution. He said he made the film when he discovered that some of his own people did not know why Hopi clowns do some of the things they do, such as stand on rooftops and urinate on tourists during certain Hopi festivals. But now he worries that he may have told too much, even though repeated cutting reduced the film's length to fifteen minutes.

Masayesva has also said, "I have come to believe that the sacred aspects of our existence that encourage the continuity and vitality of Native peoples

In this portrayal of the 1620 landing of the Pilgrims at Plymouth Rock, in present-day Massachusetts, a local Native inhabitant warily regards the newcomers. Most popular images of encounters between Indians and early settlers downplay the tensions and misunderstandings that grew around the restrictions placed on Native land by English colonizers.

are being manipulated by an aesthetic in which money is the most important qualification. This contradicts values intrinsic to what is sacred and may destroy our substance."

MASSACHUSETTS

Massachusetts became the sixth U.S. state on February 6, 1788. Its name is derived from a Native term for "Great Mountain Place." As an English colony, Massachusetts had its beginnings in 1620 with the founding of Plymouth, the second permanent English settlement in North America.

At the time of early European settlement, a number of Native peoples inhabited the area known today as New England. The Massachuset Indians, known as the People at the Big Hill, were allied with the powerful Narragansetts. They lived interior to the Patuxets (Pawtuckets) north of Shaw-

mut (Boston) and the Wampanoags. Their westerly neighbors were the Nipmucks, the Pocumtucks along the Connecticut River, and in the Berkshire-Hudson region of western Massachusetts, the Mahicans. All of these groups are culturally Algonquian.

In the early 1600s, explorers kidnapped several Patuxets and Wampanoags for display in England or to sell into slavery in Spain. Squanto, a Patuxet, is notable for surviving both of these fates, spending ten years in England. With Samoset and Massasoit, he aided the Pilgrim settlers at Plymouth.

Like Native Americans elsewhere, the Indians of Massachusetts were decimated by disease and lost their lands when trespassing settlers disregarded land-sale agreements. The Indians had assumed that these agreements governed the use of the land, not entitlement to ownership of the land. The Puritans also restricted the Indians' agriculture and hunting. The patient but doomed efforts by Metacom (King Philip) to compromise with Puritan

Wampanoag leader Massasoit is depicted forging a treaty with Pilgrim settlers at Plymouth. During the 1630s, Massasoit formed several alliances with English colonists, mostly in an effort to preserve his people's numbers and their culture.

dictates finally exploded in King Philip's War, widely devastating white settlements until Philip was slain in 1676. Captives of this war became slaves in the Caribbean and Bermuda.

Of several reservations established prior to 1700, only Hassanamesitt Nipmuck—4 acres (1.6 hectares) in Grafton—remains. The Chaubunagungamaug Nipmuck band is based at Webster. Long harrassed by Indians and whites, the Pocumtucks lost in King Philip's War and the Deerfield Raid of 1704 and eventually dispersed. The Mashpee Wampanoags are actively involved with cultural preservation issues in an effort to counter the effects of tourism on Cape Cod. They have declared Thanksgiving a day of mourning and wryly consider the Pilgrims "America's first boat people" and the first Thanksgiving "America's first welfare event."

The 1990 U.S. Census lists 12,241 Native people as residents of Massachusetts, ranking the state thirty-sixth among states in Native American population.

SEE ALSO:
Algonquian Group; King Philip's War; Massasoit; Narragansett; Samoset; Squanto.

MASSASOIT (c. 1580–1661)

A Wampanoag, Massasoit ("Yellow Feather") was among the first Native American leaders to greet English settlers in what would become Puritan New England. His people, the Wampanoags, assisted the Puritans during their first hard winters in the new land and took part in the first Thanksgiving.

Massasoit allied with the Pilgrims out of necessity; many of his people had died in an epidemic shortly before the whites arrived, and he sought to forge an alliance with them against the more numerous Narragansetts. Massasoit was described by William Bradford in 1621 as "lustie . . . in his best years, an able body grave of countenance, spare of speech, strong [and] tall." Massasoit, father of Metacom, favored friendly relations with the English colonists when he became the Wampanoags' most influential leader about 1632. His alliance with the Boston colony was maintained during the Pequot War (1636), during which all Native peoples in New England suffered large population losses. Before the war, the English immigrants were a minority in the area; after it, they were a majority.

Massasoit also helped the Puritan dissident Roger Williams, who in 1636 founded the colony that would become Rhode Island, escape arrest by Puritan authorities for his views on religious and political freedom.

As he aged, Massasoit became disillusioned with the colonists as increasing numbers of them pressed his people from their lands. Upon his death, Alexander, Massasoit's son, briefly served as grand sachem of the Wampanoags until his own death. Metacom, whom the English called "King Philip" became grand sachem after Alexander.

SEE ALSO:
King Philip's War; Massachusetts; Pequot War.

MATHER, COTTON (1663–1728)

Cotton Mather, born in Boston on February 12, 1663, was a Puritan minister and author. The Puritans had come to North America from England so they could practice their own religion. They were called Puritans because they wanted to make their church services simpler than Church of England services. Most Puritans lived in the Massachusetts Bay Colony at the mouth of the Charles River in what is now Boston.

Mather, an intelligent student and gifted orator, began his studies at Harvard College at the age of twelve. Once he became a minister, he used his power and position to develop a unique, although racist, explanation for the origin of Indians. "We may guess that probably the devil decoyed those miserable savages hither, in hopes that the gospel of the Lord Jesus Christ would never come here to destroy or disturb his absolute empire over them," he wrote in one of his many sermons.

Mather believed in disembodiment, a school of thought that accepted Indians as subhumans and treated them as objects to conquer. The massacre of the Pequot Indians during what non-Indians called the Pequot War, beginning in 1636, inspired Mather to write, ". . . no less than six hundred souls were brought down to hell that day." Mather was also an avid believer in the existence of witchcraft, which he thought was evil. His sermons helped begin a period of hysteria about witchcraft that con-

tinued throughout the American colonial period. During this time of persecution, approximately two hundred people with unpopular views, primarily women, were accused of witchcraft, hunted down, tried, and executed, often by being burned at the stake.

During his lifetime, Mather wrote and published more than four hundred works, ranging from social reform to science to American history. One of his most famous works, *Magnalia Christi Americana*, published in 1702, is a spiritual history of non-Native people in America from the founding of New England up to his own time.

Toward the end of his life, Mather's tolerance increased and his thinking shifted from the strict Puritan beliefs of the seventeenth century toward the more rationalistic ideas of the eighteenth century. Rationalism emphasizes that the exercise of reason, rather than the acceptance of authority or spiritual revelation, is the prime source of spiritual truth. Mather died in Boston on February 13, 1728.

SEE ALSO:
Pequot War.

MATHEWS, JOHN JOSEPH (1894–1979)

Osage author and historian John Joseph Mathews was born on November 16, 1894, at Pawhuska, the capital of the Osage Nation, which is now Osage County, Oklahoma. His father was a merchant who later founded the Citizen's National Bank of Pawhuska.

After 1917, when oil was discovered on Osage lands, his share of the tribal royalties allowed him financial independence for the rest of his life. He entered the University of Oklahoma in 1914, where he played football and graduated in 1920 with a degree in geology and Phi Beta Kappa honors, after having his studies interrupted by three years of service in World War I. In 1923, he took a second bachelor's degree, in natural science, from Merton College at Oxford in England and then studied at the School of International Relations in Geneva, Switzerland.

This painting, taken from the tomb of Mayan royalty, supports the belief that the ancient Mayas decorated their surroundings—and themselves—with vivid colors and intricate designs.

Dove (Christine Quintasket) had published *Cogewa, the Half-Blood* (1927), the first novel by an Indian woman.

Also in 1934, Mathews was elected to the Osage Tribal Council; he was reelected in 1938, serving eight years altogether. From his work on the council he is credited with establishing the Osage Tribal Museum in 1938. He also represented the tribe in delegations to Washington, D.C.

In 1945, Mathews published *Talking to the Moon*. In 1951, he published a biography of his lifelong friend E. W. Marland, who had been governor of Oklahoma in the 1930s, titled *Life and Death of an Oilman: The Career of E. W. Marland*.

Mathews's last book was a monumental, eight-hundred-page history of his tribe, titled *The Osages: Children of the Middle Waters*, published in 1961. He died on June 11, 1979.

SEE ALSO:
Mourning Dove.

In 1932, he published his first book, *Wah'Kon-Tah: The Osage and the White Man's Road*, based on the papers and diaries of Laban J. Miles, who had been the federal agent to the Osages in the late nineteenth century. Chosen a book club selection, the book surprisingly sold far beyond the expectations of Mathews and his publisher, the University of Oklahoma Press. In 1934, Mathews published his first novel, *Sundown*, not long after Mourning

MAYA

To many of the scholars who have studied them, the Mayas remain a subject of mystery and speculation. Scholars once speculated that the Mayas were relatively peaceful, but history, as revealed in the Mayas' own recently deciphered writing, now portrays them as warlike. For fifteen centuries, the Mayas also made some of the most inhospitable jungles in the world bloom with corn—what the Mayas called "the sunbeams of the gods"—the basic food for a civilization that in many respects was a match for any in the so-called Old World.

According to author Howard La Fay, "Gone forever is the image of the Maya as peaceful, rather primitive farmers practicing esoteric religious rites in their jungle fastness. What emerges is a portrait of a vivid, warlike race, numerous beyond any previous estimate, employing sophisticated agricultural techniques. And like the Vikings half a world away, they traded and raided with zest." The major Mayan urban areas, each with its distinctive customs, language, and art forms, vied for dominance.

In more than one hundred cities, Mayan artists produced some of the most exquisite art in the world of their time, while Mayan scientists calculated solar and lunar eclipses with an accuracy that would not be excelled until modern times. The Mayan calendar calculated the year more accurately than the Roman calendar that we use today. The Mayas also calculated the path of Venus and were the first to develop a concept of negative numbers in mathematics. Yet, by the time the first Spanish explorers reached Mesoamerica (Central America), Mayan civilization was crumbling, probably from incessant warfare and overusing the land and its resources.

Unlike the Europeans, Mayas developed remarkable precision in timekeeping and astronomy because such science served their religious beliefs. And, unlike Europeans, the Mayas thought of history as cyclical. Events experienced in the past were expected to recur. A person who knew the past was believed to be able to predict the future. Success in predicting such natural phenomena as eclipses was said to be divine proof of this. Time was seen as one immutable stream,

This temple, which holds several masonry altars, graces the Mayan ruins at Altun Ha, along the coast of Belize. At its height, around 600 to 900 C.E., Mayan civilization dominated parts of southern Mexico and most of Belize and Guatemala.

These tapestries, the work of modern Mayan craftspeople of Guatemala, are popular with tourists in markets throughout Central America and in North American specialty shops as well.

stretching back to a date corresponding to August 11, 3114 B.C.E., the first date on the Mayas' "long-count" calendar.

At the height of their civilization, about 600 to 900 C.E., the Mayas dominated most of what is today southern Mexico, Guatemala, and Belize. Their civilization was not an organized empire in the Inca, Roman, or Aztec sense; many of its sites were connected by trade routes The ramparts of fortress-like Tulum looked out over the ragged surf of the Yucatán shore, gateway to a network of trading routes that connected such Mayan cities as Copán, Tikal, Chichén Itzá, and Palenque.

The origins of the Mayas are not known to contemporary scholars, aside from speculation that aspects of their culture may have been inherited from the Olmecs, who may have spoken a language related to one or more of the Mayan languages. Some evidence exists that the Mayas may have begun the building of their civilization in Kami-

naljuyu, which is today part of Guatemala City, before 1100 B.C.E. by the European calendar.

Tikal, the largest of the Mayas' many cities, was well developed by the time of Christ's birth. By the time of its height, eight hundred years later, Tikal's population was between thirty thousand and sixty thousand. The city rambled over twenty-three square miles (sixty square kilometers), while imperial Rome, which was more densely populated, covered only one-third as much area. Tikal's three thousand structures included six pyramids, seven temple palaces, and several artificial reservoirs, all covering an area of at least one square mile (2.6 square kilometers). The city is still an impressive sight, even in its decayed state, with remains of the pyramids towering two hundred feet (sixty-one meters) into the air, connected by wide causeways.

Tikal's location took advantage of a nearby portage between rivers leading to the Gulf of Mex-

This woman carries on a legacy of Mayan artistry as she makes tapestries at her home in Guatemala.

This detail is from a mural at Chichén Itzá, an ancient Mayan city in central Yucatán, Mexico, that is believed to have thrived between 514 and 1194 C.E. The illustration, which depicts a Mayan river settlement, was created during a period of resurgence for the Mayan culture in Chichén Itzá lasting for about two hundred years after 1000 C.E.

ico and the Caribbean Sea. Like most of the other Mayan cities, Tikal declined about 890 C.E. according to the history recorded on its monuments. The religious and scientific elite collapsed, and squatters moved onto the ceremonial plazas, amid the temples, living among piles of their own refuse, as the jungle reclaimed the city's outskirts. At the end of the Mayan Classic Period, there was extensive soil loss, massive erosion, a long-term decline in rainfall, and probably a number of highly communicable diseases.

Before their society collapsed from ecological exhaustion, war, or other causes, the Mayas surrounded themselves with decoration, on their buildings, as well as their bodies. William Brandon provided a word-picture of how the Mayas looked: "They tattooed their bodies and painted them red—priests were painted blue, warriors black and red, prisoners striped black and white. They occasionally filed their teeth. They distended their

pierced earlobes with . . . ear plugs, and pierced the septum of the nose to insert carved 'jewels.' They flattened their foreheads and made themselves, if they could, cross-eyed, cross-eyes being considered beautiful. They decorated themselves with feathers, breeding birds in aviaries for the most gorgeous plumes, and men wore brilliant little obsidian mirrors hanging in their long hair."

As scholars learn more about Mayan society, they have discovered that although a marked general decline occurred at about 900 C.E., it was not uniform. From time to time, new cultural infusions (mainly from the north, including the Valley of Mexico) seemed to cause some centers to rise again. For example, Chichén Itzá saw the rise of a new dynasty that included both Maya and Toltec elements for roughly two centuries after 1000 C.E.

Smallpox and repeated attempts at invasion and colonization broke the Mayas only slowly. One ill-fated Spanish expedition after another was repulsed from Maya country. In 1511, a Spanish ship en route from Panama to Santo Domingo sank off the east coast of the Yucatán, whereupon its entire ragged starving crew was captured by Natives along the coast.

Pedro de Alvarado marched from the Valley of Mexico to Guatemala in 1523 with four hundred Spanish soldiers and as many as twenty thousand Native allies, blazing a path of terror through Maya country, brutalizing and killing local inhabitants, including women, children, and infants. Still, the majority of the Mayas fought a ceaseless guerilla war that drove the Spanish from Yucatán in 1536. In 1541, after the Spanish forged alliances with some of the Mayas, and after famine, pestilence, and the ravages of civil war, the Mayas finally fell. In the centuries that followed, the Native populations of Central America have lived under the rule of various regimes following the Spanish conquest.

In Guatemala late in the twentieth century, subjugation now approaching five hundred years continues in a bloody and intractable civil war that has, for political reasons, been killing an average of 10 people a day for more than thirty years. The death toll of 138,000 people includes 100,000 murdered for political reasons and 38,000 more "disappeared." The war, in a country that is still 60 percent Mayan, follows the race and class lines of the original *conquista* ("conquest"), in which a mestizo (or Spanish-speaking) landed class brutally holds down a poverty-stricken Mayan majority.

— B. E. Johansen

SEE ALSO:

Aztec; Central America, Indigenous Peoples of; Mexico, Indigenous Peoples of; New Spain; Olmec; Spain; Toltec.

SUGGESTED READINGS:

Denevan, William, ed. *The Native Population of the Americas.* Madison: University of Wisconsin Press, 1976.

Henderson, John S. *The World of the Ancient Maya.* Ithaca, NY: Cornell University Press, 1981.

Kelley, David H. *Deciphering the Maya Script.* Austin: University of Texas Press, 1976.

Lovell, George. *Conquest and Survival in Colonial Guatemala: A Historical Geography of the Cuchu-matan Highlands, 1500–1821.* Montreal: McGill-Queen's University Press, 1985.

Recinos, Adrian, and Delia Goetz, trans. *The Annals of the Cakchiquels.* Norman: University of Oklahoma Press, 1953.

Roys, Ralph L. *The Book of Chilam Balam of Chumayel.* Norman: University of Oklahoma Press, 1967.

Wright, Ronald. *Stolen Continents: America Through Indian Eyes Since 1492.* Boston: Houghton Mifflin, 1992.

McCLINTOCK, WALTER
(1870–1949)

Walter McClintock, born on April 25, 1870, was a white man who lived and traveled with the Blackfeet during the late nineteenth and early twentieth centuries. The Blackfeet are an Algonquian tribe whose territory ranged through western Montana and adjacent southern Canada. They are divided into three main groups—the Siksika, Kainah, and Piegan.

McClintock was one of three popular authors (the other two were George B. Grinnell and J. W. Schultz) whose works brought the Blackfeet to international prominence around the turn of the century. During this period—when romantic ideas about the American Wild West were prevalent—he helped distinguish the Blackfeet as real people through descriptions of their daily life and customs.

As part of a government expedition recommending a national policy for the United States Forest Reserves, now known as the Forest Service, McClintock first visited the Blackfeet reservation in northern Montana in 1896. On this trip, he established a close friendship with the Piegan Chief Mad Wolf, who adopted McClintock as his son. McClintock continued to observe the tribe on numerous trips to the reservation during the next fifteen years.

His first volume, *The Old North Trail*, was published in England in 1910. He rewrote the book thirteen years later for a U.S. edition titled *Old Indian Trails*. He also produced many scholarly books, articles, and pamphlets on the Blackfeet Indians, almost all of which are revisions of his original work.

McClintock, Walter

Old Indian Trails is a mixture of stories, legends, and descriptions of religious rituals, mixed together with accounts of his personal experiences with the Blackfeet. He also describes the tribe's daily life and social customs, including many of their songs, and catalogs the names, uses, and preparations of herbs and medicinal plants. McClintock died in 1949.

SEE ALSO:
Algonquian Group; Blackfeet.

McDONALD, JAMES LAWRENCE
(c. 1804–1831)

James Lawrence McDonald became the first Choctaw to be admitted to the practice of law. He was a brilliant young man who, at the age of fourteen, was sent east to be privately educated by the Reverend Dr. Carnahan, later the president of Princeton College. While studying with Dr. Carnahan, McDonald was a ward in the home of Thomas L. McKinney, who later became commissioner of Indian Affairs. When he was done studying with Carnahan, he was sent to Ohio, where he studied law in the office of Judge John McLean, later a justice of the United States Supreme Court.

After being admitted to the bar, McDonald returned to Choctaw country to visit his mother. There, he was appointed to the Choctaw delegation, which departed in 1824 for Washington, D.C. Led by famed Choctaw negotiator and orator Pushmataha, the delegation set out to negotiate the agreement that eventually became the Treaty of 1825 between the Choctaws and the United States.

In this agreement, the United States sought to buy back from the Choctaws a portion of the land west of the Mississippi River that it had sold to the Choctaws in the Treaty of 1820. This land now comprises the southwestern portion of the state of Arkansas. At the negotiations for the Treaty of 1820, the Choctaws told General Andrew Jackson that the land the United States wanted to sell them was already occupied by some U.S. squatters. Pushmataha inquired of Jackson what was to be done with them, and Jackson promised to send U.S.

troops to drive them out. By 1824, however, the United States was seeking to buy back that piece of land rather than forcibly evict the Arkansas squatters.

Before the 1824–1825 delegation arrived in Washington, the Choctaw Nation lost one of its three district chiefs when Puckshenubbe, Great Medal Mingo (a formal title of rank) of the Okla Falaya tribal division, died in Memphis, Tennessee. After arriving in Washington, Pushmataha, Great Medal Mingo of the Okla Hannali tribal division and the most influential Choctaw of his generation, fell ill and died of the croup on December 24, 1824.

The loss of these two great leaders was devastating to the Choctaws, and they turned to James Lawrence McDonald to take over the negotiations. It may have been the first instance in United States–Indian relations when Indians were represented by one of their own people trained in the law. Secretary of State John C. Calhoun and Thomas McKinney, commissioner of Indian Affairs, found McDonald to be a worthy adversary. McKinney wrote, "I found him so skilled in the business of his mission . . . as to make it more of an up-hill business than I had ever before experienced in negotiating with Indians. I believe Mr. Calhoun thought so too."

McDonald refused to negotiate with the U.S. representatives until the United States had settled all of the outstanding claims that the Choctaws held against the United States. The U.S. delegates had anticipated a quick agreement in which the Choctaws would cede more of their land for very little compensation; they found McDonald's demands exasperating. He refused to relent, however. To get the agreement it sought, the United States was forced to relinquish $14,972.50 that it had owed to the Choctaws for a decade as payment for Choctaw military participation in General Jackson's Pensacola campaign against the Seminoles. The government was also forced to pay $2,000 for damages suffered by individual Choctaws from U.S. citizens.

For the failure of the United States to provide a blacksmith to the Choctaws, as had been stipulated in an earlier treaty, McDonald forced the U.S. treaty commissioners to forgive all of the outstanding debt of individual Choctaws to the feder-

862

al trading house on the Tombigbee River in the Choctaw country. To resolve other outstanding claims and make it possible, finally, to get negotiations underway, the United States agreed to pay the Choctaws $6,000 dollars annually for a period of sixteen years.

Finally, in exchange for ceding the land—the motivating factor for the United States' inviting the Choctaws to enter into the negotiations—McDonald demanded and received a much higher price than the Americans had intended to pay. The Choctaws were to be paid six thousand dollars annually, forever, with the payments for the first twenty years to be applied to the support of a school system for the Choctaw Nation. Furthermore, the Choctaws demanded that the United States survey the new eastern boundary for the Choctaw lands and remove all U.S. citizens who might be found on the Choctaw side of the line. The United States fulfilled this obligation, and American squatters were evicted by the army.

In November 1826, McDonald was a member of the Choctaw delegation at treaty negotiations in the Choctaw country at which the United States sought to get the Choctaws to remove to their western lands. The Choctaw delegation refused to even discuss removal with the U.S. commissioners, and the negotiations ended without a treaty. This helped postpone a Choctaw removal treaty for another four years.

— D. L. Birchfield.

SEE ALSO:
Choctaw; Pushmataha; Removal Act, Indian.

McGILLIVRAY, ALEXANDER
(c. 1759–1793)

Alexander McGillivray became principal chief of the Muscogee Confederation (Creeks) during the late eighteenth century and signed the first treaty between the Creeks and the United States in 1790 in New York City. He was born about 1759 in today's Elmore County, Alabama, in the Upper Creek village of Tallassee on the Coosa River. His father was a wealthy Scots trader, and his mother was of Creek and French descent.

At the age of fourteen, he was sent to South Carolina to be tutored by a relative. His education then continued by apprenticeship in a mercantile establishment in Savannah, Georgia. He returned to the Creek country well prepared for a career in business, politics, and diplomacy.

When McGillivray was only about eighteen years old, he became principal leader of the Upper Creeks when Emistesequo transferred his leadership role to him. A few years later, at a grand council of the leaders of the Creek villages in 1783, he was elected principal chief and head warrior of the nation. His skill at diplomacy and his education, a critical necessity in dealing with the European colonial powers, accounted for his rapid rise to leadership of the nation.

He sided with the British during the American Revolution, and afterward he worked tirelessly to try to halve the encroachments onto Creek lands by United States citizens, especially by Georgians. He formed alliances with the Spanish in Florida, and he also became a partner in the trading firm of Panton, Leslie & Company, based in Pensacola. In 1790, he led a Creek delegation to the United States capitol, then in New York City, where he met with the United States Senate and signed the first treaty between the two nations.

During his life, he became a wealthy merchant and planter who owned sixty slaves and three hundred head of cattle. At various times, he received annual stipends of $1,200 from the United States and $3,500 from Spain, and he held commissions as a colonel in the Spanish army, a brigadier general in the United States Army, and a general in the British army. He died February 17, 1793, in Pensacola, Florida, of natural causes.

SEE ALSO:
Creek.

McINTOSH, WILLIAM
(c. 1775–1825)

William McIntosh became the principal leader of the Lower Creek villages of the Muscogee Confederation. He sided with the United States in the War of 1812 and led the Lower Creeks in war

William McIntosh as he appeared to an artist portraying the Lower Creek leader in a style befitting both his combined Scots-Creek ancestry and his alliance with the United States around the time of the War of 1812.

Tecumseh. When the War of 1812 broke out, pitting the British and Tecumseh's Indian alliance against the United States and its Indian allies, McIntosh was commissioned a major general in the United States Army. He led Lower Creek troops against the Upper Creeks at the Battle of Atasi in 1813 and at the decisive Battle of Horseshoe Bend in 1814, where the Upper Creeks, who were known as Red Sticks, were crushed.

At the end of the war, because some of the Creeks had sided with the British, U. S. General Andrew Jackson demanded that the Creeks cede 22 million acres (8.8 million hectares) of their national territory to the United States. Afterward, the Creek national council decreed the death penalty for any Creek leader who signed any further treaties of land cession.

McIntosh, however, believed that the removal of the Creeks to land west of the Mississippi River was inevitable and that the United States would eventually seize all Creek lands in the Southeast. He believed it was better to get money for the land while the tribe could do so. Accordingly, he signed land cession treaties in 1818, 1821, and 1825. The Creek national council condemned him to death, and the execution was carried out by a delegation led by McIntosh's old Upper Creek rival, Menawa, on May 1, 1825, as McIntosh tried to flee from his house.

SEE ALSO:

Creek; Jackson, Andrew; Removal Act, Indian; Tecumseh.

against the Upper Creeks, who had joined with Tecumseh and the British in the War of 1812.

He was born about 1775 in present-day Carroll County in western Georgia, in the important Lower Creek village of Coweta. His father, a Scots captain in the British army, was the British agent to the Creeks, and his mother was a Creek woman.

McIntosh rose to prominence among the Lower Creeks when he opposed Tecumseh's appeal to the Creeks in 1811 to join the pan-Indian alliance that the Shawnee leader was trying to form. Many of the Upper Creeks, under the leadership of Menawa, became ardent followers of